Th

An account (
Visit to East Africa and His Divine Discourses

By

Sri. N. Kasturi

Publications Division

PRASANTHI NILAYAM

SRI SATHYA SAI SADHANA TRUST,
Publications Division
Prasanthi Nilayam - 515 134
Anantapur District, Andhra Pradesh, INDIA
STD: 08555 ISD: 91-8555 Phone: 287375 Fax: 287236
E-mail: orders@sssbpt.org

ISBN: 978-93-5069-090-1

First Edition: July 2014

Published by

The Convener,
Sri Sathya Sai Sadhana Trust, Publications Division
Prasanthi Nilayam, India, Pin Code - 515134
STD : 08555 ISD: 91-8555   Phone: 287375 Fax: 287236

Printed at

Createspace

Table Of Contents

PART I - THE LIGHT OF LOVE

(An account of the Visit of Bhagawan Sri Sathya Sai Baba to East Africa)

PART II - DISCOURSES OF BABA

(Discourses Of Bhagawan Sri Sathya Sai Baba In East Africa)

Part I

An account of the Visit of Bhagawan Sri Sathya Sai Baba to East Africa from 30th June, 1968 to 14th July, 1968.

1.

Across The Sea

"My Reality is unreachable. It will be unreachable not only today, but even for a thousand years; though the thousand years are spent in ardent inquiry by all the people of the world, acting in unison. But, the Bliss emanating from that Reality, that is conferred by that Reality is within the reach of all the nations of the earth, and you can partake of it... Men have failed to recognise Me, for I am enveloped in humanness. My Reality is this: This is a human form, worn by the One Divine Principle that manifests Itself as all the God-Forms adored by Man... This Sathya Sai Manifestation is Divine Reality Itself. You are fortunate that you can grasp this Truth, not at some future date when the Human Frame has been discarded, but luckily, even while It is with you, before you. You will soon be awarded the joy of witnessing the declaration by all people's of the Divinity of this Sathya Sai Manifestation."

This Announcement made at a gathering of 1200 delegates from all over the world, on the 17th of May, 1968, reverberated from shore to shore of every sea, from mountain to mountain on every land. Africa shared in that acclamation and yearned that the chance to adore might soon be vouchsafed to her. Baba responded to that yearning. For, the very next moment, He followed up this Declaration with the statement, "The people of East Africa have already sought My grace and made arrangements for My visit to that part of the World, next month!"

On the last day of June, 1968, the visit to East Africa fructified! On that historic day at Bombay, Baba had also said, "I have resolved to enfold in the fostering care of the universal *dharma* laid down in the Vedas, the peoples of the world. This will be done soon. This is My task. It is not My task to spread awe and wonder in the world by My power and draw men to Me thereby. I shall sustain Truth and uproot untruth. I shall render you happy and ecstatic, in the splendour of that Triumph." The visit was, therefore, epoch-making; it marked the opening of a golden chapter in the history of humanity, of an era of love, humility, and reverence, of earnestness, discipline, and devotion in man's march towards his future.

Though Baba has declared that the whole world is His mansion and that each continent is but a hall in that mansion, and though He said that His visit to Africa was but a peep into one of the rooms of that mansion, His devotees in India and other countries felt the deeper significance of the occasion and were thrilled with genuine joy. Thousands gathered at the Airport, Bangalore, when Baba emplaned to Bombay, on 28th June. They sang *bhajans* in chorus and surged around with the homage of flower garlands in their hands. Baba accepted the homage and curbed their boundless enthusiasm, with a few words of advice. Bhagawan Sri Sathya Sai Seva Samiti, Bombay had announced a public meeting and *bhajan* sessions at Dharmakshetra, when representatives of Sathya Sai Organisations and others could offer homage at the Lotus Feet. The meeting started at 6 p.m. Hon'ble Sri. P. K. Savant, Minister and President, Sri Sathya Sai Prasanthi Vidwanmahasabha, Maharashtra, spoke a few words about Baba's visit to Africa. "Baba is present always and everywhere. His Message has also reached every nook and corner of the world, as was evident during the world conference. Now, Baba is proceeding in concrete Form to give His Love and His Light to the peoples of the countries beyond the sea. Many persons have gone from India to the West in the past, and given the West a great understanding of the culture of this land. Baba is the embodiment of love, the wisdom, and the power that are enshrined in all the religions of the world. So, this series of visits to other countries will create lasting goodwill and brotherliness between all the nations of the world. We pray that Baba sends us His blessings from Africa, where His physical Presence will be for some days. We dare not felicitate; we can never think of a 'send-off'; we can only express our jubilation at the decision of Baba; we have in our minds only the idea of welcoming Him into our hearts and homes. We pray for blessings and His protecting and guiding Hand."

Members of the *bhajan* units of Bombay city, students of the balvikas (moral instruction classes run by the Samiti), and others garlanded Baba. Shri Savant, Shri Bharde (Speaker, Legislative Assembly, Bombay), Shri Page (Chairman, Legislative Council, Bombay), Shri Durgadas Khanna (Chairman, Legislative Council, Punjab), and many others offered homage to Baba. More than 20,000 citizens of Bombay had *darshan* of Baba at the meeting. In His infinite grace, Baba moved among the thickly packed gathering and received the flowers with which the devotees desired to indicate their joy.

On the 30th, the vast terrace of the main building of the Santa Cruz Airport spilled over with thousands of devotees, who had secured standing space thereon, so that they may have the *darshan* of Baba when He comes to embark the Air India Boeing, which leaves at 9 a.m. on the direct flight to Nairobi. Hundreds of enterprising men and women braved official frowns and the fierce glare of the ground staff, and succeeded in entering the area around the plane. Baba walked the length of the building, waving His hand, so that the cheering masses atop it could imprint that charming picture in their hearts. Seated in the plane, Baba was approached by the pilots and the crew, as well as by some high officers of the Indian Airlines. He graciously blessed them all, giving to quite a few the unique gift of *vibhuti*, created on the spot for each by a wave of His divine hand.

During the flight, Baba continued this mission of grace. Many passengers recognised Him and asked for the grant of the precious chance of few words with Him. Others came to know of Him and hurried to benefit themselves in a similar manner. While the plane was 35,000 feet above the Arabian Sea, flying at 590 miles an hour, many had the chance of sitting next to Baba and after conversing with Him, got His precious autograph, too. In spite of the monsoon and a bit of 'rough weather', which the plane had to encounter for a few minutes, the passage to Africa was quite comfortable. The sea appeared from that height a calm sheet, with an occasional quiver of foam; one scarcely felt the speed. We felt as if we sat in a plush theatre, waiting for the curtain to rise and the play to begin. The curtain was to rise in Nairobi and the play was to be *'Love Lit Large'*, the same that was enacted in every place that had won the chance of a visit by Baba.

Baba had a charming sense of humour, which springs from divine detachment, and the continuous consciousness of His being the director of the play. He wrote during the flight, post cards for the little tots, whom He wanted to surprise by the missiles; He wrote and got delivered a post card to the Raymers of U.S.A. They were members of His party and were occupying seats in the row just before His, giving His own address as 'Boeing 707'. Bob Raymer responded in the same spirit of neighbourliness, sending Baba a post card in reply, with the lines, "The sky is blue; the ocean too; Our wish has come true. We are flying with you!" Baba enjoyed the quickness and the aptness of the reply. Meanwhile, the plane had crossed the shore and was flying over reddish yellow barrenness, with slender streaks and dark blotches to relieve the monotony. Vast fluffs of white cloud soon hid the ground. Mount Kenya was announced, as the name of the peak we saw on our right, popping its sharp head over the Sea of Milk. When our watches indicated 2:24 p.m., we had come under the clouds, over a quilt of green vegetation, with hundreds of gleaming roofs reflecting the rays of the sun, and the plane made a perfect landing on the tarmac at Embaksi Airport, at four minutes to twelve, local time.

2.

'Nandalala' At Nairobi

Nairobi was astir, since morning, for news had spread that Bhagawan was coming over the Sea. Cheering masses were gathered on the terrace of the aerodrome building; when they saw Baba alighting, their joy knew no bounds. Baba was received near the plane by Dr. Chhotabhai G. Patel of Kampala, whose persistence and prayers, on behalf of the peoples of East Africa, had won for the continent this great good fortune. Dr. Patel drove Baba to the open spaces behind the airport, where a huge gathering of Nairobians were waiting and engaging themselves in *bhajan, Nandalala! Nandalala!* While the members of His party were going through the routine hurdles, in the halls and corridors of the international airport; Baba had begun, within minutes of His arrival in Africa, His mission of mercy, His mission of spreading happiness and joy.

It was difficult to decide, whether the *bhajan*s they sang with such sweetness were echoes from India or whether the *bhajan*s sung in India were echoes of the songs from Africa. And, the devotion that rang true in every turn of tone, in every wave of sound, through every beat of time! In a letter written to Dr. Gokak, Vice-chancellor, University of Bangalore, Baba characterised it thus, "It was feast for the eye, the scene when they scattered flowers and waved lights. They sang so melodiously, so sincerely, that I was reminded of the days of Jayadeva and Gauranga! Those, who had come with Me (Kasturi) from India shed tears of joy, at the thrilling enthusiasm of that mammoth gathering. They had seldom seen such supreme moments of grateful ecstasy in India."

We had to proceed to Kampala, 407 miles away, by car and so, the cars sped on, along the well-laid road. Baba was in the car of Dr. Patel. The rest followed at some distance. The scenery around was delicious, for vegetation was green and plentiful on both sides of the road, for miles and miles. The road leaped gracefully, over hill after hill, rising from 5500 feet at Nairobi to even 9000 feet and coming down to 7000 at Eldoret and rising up again to 4000 at Kampala. The awe-inspiring sight of the famous Rift Valley, 2000 feet below, down a sheet escarpment, more than thirty miles broad and stretching far into the North and South, is one of the free gifts this road provides. By the side of Lake Nakuru, in this valley lies the town of Nakuru, where devotees of Baba had assembled in the house of Mr. Thakur, the ex-Mayor, awaiting the arrival of their Master and Lord. They were engaged in *bhajan*, for they knew that nothing can draw divinity into the heart as quickly and as firmly as the contemplation on the might and majesty of God. In spite of the fact that He had still 310 miles to go, before some rest could be given to the body, Baba responded to the pining hearts and alighted at the place. He sat for some time receiving the adoration and blessed the people, who had gathered. And, the journey was resumed.

There was a freshness and a joy in the air, a fragrance of sincere achievement the ozone of a free, determined intellect and the music of the motto of Kenya, "Harambee," "Let's all pull together!" We saw vast valleys green with wheatfields, kept free from pests by low flying insecticide spraying aircraft. We saw thick plantations of wattle; we passed through cattle farms and dairy colonies. The velvet verdure was pleasing; the coolness of the air was comforting. The rains that come upon this land during all months of the year have mothered many gurgling streams and fresh water lakes, which beautify the landscape and fructify the soil.

At Eldoret, 83 miles from Nakuru, citizens welcomed Baba on the outskirts of the town, for He could not alight and give *darshan* to the huge gathering that had assembled inside the town; Baba sped along. The entry into the state of Uganda was marked by a new type of welcome. The state had provided Baba with a pilot car, from Malaba, on the frontier, as a sign and symbol of His honoured status, a symbol that was to be with Him throughout His stay in the State. Then, the cars drove along to Jinja, where the Nile river flows out of Lake Victoria, to fulfil its arduous vow to reach the Mediterranean Sea. At Owen Falls near Jinja, where the Nile is persuaded to "begin its long and beneficent journey to the sea, by leaping through a turbine," we have the power station that feeds the factories and machinery of the entire East Africa. Here too, the devotees had the unique chance of *darshan*.

3.

Welcome To Uganda

At last, Kampala was reached at about 1:30 a.m. Wide banners of silken welcome streamed across the roads, at Nairobi, and other towns enroute, until at last, they increased in number and splendour as the suburbs of Kampala were neared. Many of them were illuminated signs of welcome, because Baba was to pass under them at night. They referred to Him as Bhagawan and hailed His arrival with joy and gratitude. One of us said that they were 108 in number, but we did not verify whether it was divine will that made it so. Another feature that was cool to the eye and flattering to our culture was the liberal use of plantain stems, with their broad green leaves for decorating each post and pillar and arch. Later, we discovered that the plantain was a very important dish in all African lunches and dinners.

Dr. Patel erected a temporary 'hall' with corrugated roofing, in the open space before his house; here. About 2000 people awaited Baba, even in the late hour, singing *bhajans* since hours with unabated earnestness, Indians and Africans together. Baba went straight into the 'hall', gave *darshan* for some minutes to the thirsty eyes and then, retired into the house. Kampala did not sleep that night, for the citizens longed for daybreak, when they could see Baba, who had brought to them the hope and the courage that the all-knowing Father alone can impart.

Streams of pilgrims to the Lotus feet soon filled the 'hall' that Dr. Patel had erected from the anticipated gathering. Within a few hours after sunrise on the final day of July, the tarpaulins covering the sides had to be removed, to give more and more people the chance to 'see' Baba, when He sat on the chair placed in the centre, while *bhajan* was being sung in chorus by thousands of devotees. Baba blessed the men and women, who sang in earnest sincerity, in a well organised, concerted manner. He came down from the chair and moved along the passages between the blocks, where the people were seated, showering upon each the glance of divine compassion. Now and then, He stopped, facing the massed throng of yearning hearts. When His attention was drawn by a sad or sick face, a dispirited or distressed individual - Baba is the Indweller of all, He knows the innermost mystery of everyone. He stood for a moment in front of that person, waved His hand gently for a while, and, catching with His fingers the divine cure that He created on the spot (generally, it is *vibhuti* or potent Holy Ash), He placed it in the palm of the recipient or applied it on his brow or directed him to swallow it, then or later. We felt that those were the anguished hearts that prevailed upon Baba to travel across the sea, so that they might imbibe health and strength through His personal ministration.

The inspector general of Police in Uganda, Mr. Oryema paid his respects to Baba that morning and was very happy to receive from Baba blessings and signs of grace. The Chief of Staff of the Uganda Army, General Iddyamin came later, with his family, and had a long conversation with Baba. He was delighted at the grace that 'the great spiritual leader of the East' bestowed on him; during the interviews, he must have received intimations of the Omnipresence and Omniscience of Baba, as all who are privileged to receive it do. Baba was engaged in this Task of satisfying the cravings of the spirit in man and alleviating the grief of man, during all hours of the day and night, at Kampala - as He is, everywhere, at all times. When someone suggested that Baba might drive around the city and 'see' the architecture of some of the new buildings and some of the 'sights', Baba replied, "I have no need to see the place; I am here always. You may drive around. I have My work, the work for which I have come."

That evening, however, the Trustees of the 'Sanathana Dharma Samaj of Kampala' were able to persuade Him to visit the temple. The Indian Community of Kampala had gathered there in large numbers, for *darshan*. Baba went to the temple at 6 p.m. and, after witnessing arati at the shrines of Shiva, Rama, and Krishna, He sang a few *bhajans* and filled the hearts of the thousands, who were gathered there, with unforgettable sweetness.

Returning from the temple, Baba drove up the hill, which carries the television tower, and while coming down, He stopped for a while to bless an african police constable, who came to Him seeking His blessings. Baba created for him a charming locket, with the picture of Christ (he was a Christian by faith, we learnt later) imprinted on it. Baba has come to strengthen the faith of each person in the religion that he was established himself in; His *dharma* is all-inclusive. On Shivaratri day, 1966, Baba announced as the emblem of the *dharma* that He has to resuscitate, a five-starred circle, with the symbols of Christianity, Islam, Zoroastrianism, Buddhism, and Hinduism in each star and Lotus of the Heart in the centre. His teachings are universal and applicable to seekers and aspirants of all faiths. In East Africa, too, He created and gifted as a sign of grace, holy articles to many, according to the religion that each professed. His Love knows no barriers, recognises no boundaries, between 'ism and ism'.

Baba gave special instructions that everyone, who comes, must be called in and seated comfortably during *bhajan* and that the disabled and the sick must be tended with fond affection by volunteers and all concerned. On 2nd July, while going round the lines of squatting people, Baba called for special interview a large number of such persons, rich and poor, old and young, Indian and African. In fact, one could see that Africans were more in number than the rest. They were all taken inside the gate and seated before the room, where the interviews were granted. Baba Himself called in those, whom He wanted next, sometimes leading them by the hand Himself into the room. Everyone, who emerged, had a smile on the face, a ray of hope in the heart, a core of courage in the head, a lighter step, and a brighter eye. Two patients - a polio affected boy and a young man, who was moved about in a wheeled chair - struck wonder into the hearts of the vast multitudes outside, when they walked briskly along after going into Baba's room, decrepit and helpless! It was also discovered that one stalwart person was selected by Baba for treatment. Everyone around him wondered why he had been asked by Baba to join the queue - he was stone deaf and when he came out of the room, he could for the first time experience the amazing world of speech and sound!

While listening to the various engagements that were proposed for Him during His stay in Kampala, Baba suggested in the afternoon, that those, who are genuinely interested in sadhana or spiritual practices, must be encouraged to proceed forward from wherever they are. They must be made aware of the pitfalls that lay in their path; they must be warned against conceit or self-satisfaction or even listlessness and despair. Therefore, Dr. Patel said that he would ask some of them, who were praying for 'interviews' with Baba to meet Him on a fixed day and time. Such is the grace that Baba is ever willing to shower on aspirants, trekking along any path to God. Those, who practise in their daily lives the disciplines that will lead them to peace and enlightenment, are the salt of the earth, the vital sap.

In the evening, after the *bhajan* sessions, when He gave *darshan* to thousands, Baba drove up the hill, on which is built the Bahai house of worship. Returning, Baba spoke about the fundamental unity of all religions. The rites and ritualism, the forms and formalities might differ and have to differ; but, the object of every religion is to cleanse the mind of ego and the false attachment that the ego develops to the body, the senses, and the objects of the external world. Baba, however, said that, while speaking about the fundamental unity, we should not try to insist on uniformity, nor raise the all-religions-are-one-faith into a new faith in opposition to the faiths, whose unity it is proposed to establish! Let the different faiths exist, let them prosper, let them be practised more effectively, let the praise of God be sung in all languages, in a variety of tunes - that should be the ideal. We understood then, why, in Baba's symbolism, the sign for each religion had an independent status around the blooming lotus of the heart, from which the flame of knowledge-realisation was leaping forth.

Reaching Dr. Patel's place about 8:30 p.m., Baba was surprised that the gathering had not dispersed, but was still engaged in *bhajan* in the hope that Baba would come again into its midst and give them another *darshan*. In fact, the sight of that face with a thousand moods, all resplendent with compassion and love, is never fully satisfying. You might be seated in front of Him for hours, but immediately, when you rise to leave, you are tempted to sit again and drink in the charm. Baba not only went into the 'hall', He moved among the ranks. He selected a few 'patients' for interview, too; and spent about an hour, ministering to their ills and prescribing remedies and granting them His invaluable blessings. Perhaps, they had come from long distances and

could not stay overnight, for reasons He sympathised with!
Or, their yearning to see Him and to sweeten their lives with
His Love was so overpowering!

4.

The Wisdom Of The Wild

On the 3rd day of July, we had a very busy schedule. First, the flight to Ngorongoro crater, 310 miles away in Tanzania, described as "the greatest permanent concentration of wild life in Africa, in a setting of unequalled grandeur". Reaching the Entebbe International Airport (21 miles) by car, Baba and His party boarded a twin-engine aircraft, specially chartered, at 7:15 a.m., while three of us followed Him in a single-engine Super Skywagon. Until 8:35 a.m., we were flying over the Lake Victoria, the cradle of the Nile, an immense area of fresh water, 250 miles long and 1509 miles wide, situated at a height of 4000 feet, above the sea level. The waters of the Lake were giggling good-humouredly when we looked down upon them from our frail vehicle, whirring along on a single heart. Here and there, we noticed silver carpets with fluffy edges, where the morning sun spread his rays. There were small islands with dark green shores, but the shore of the lake was lost in the distant blue. The pilot told us that we were flying over the Serengeti National Park, best known for its magnificent lions. He alerted us to watch out for gazelle, zebra, and wildebeest (S. Afr.), a gnu, of which species hundreds of thousands live in that area. We were rewarded by the sight of a few herds of antelopes and zebras from a height of 7000 feet. At 9-15 a.m., the aircraft landed on the airstrip, right inside the Crater, by the side of a vast Lake, with millions of flamingoes gambolling flamboyantly on the shore.

Baba had reached a few minutes earlier and a plane chartered at Nairobi brought Bob Raymer and others from that city a few minutes later. The crater is a vast level of circular plain, once the mouth of a gigantic volcano, but now the escarpment alone remains to mark out of the area of 127 square miles of grassland, bush, and forest, sheltering large masses of wild life, and a few Masi herdsmen too, tending cattle in this fantastic milieu. We went up to the Crater Lodge in Land Rover, seeing a small group of elephants on the way and one solitary ostrich. Coming down the escarpment from the lodge an hour later, we drove into wild buffaloes, and gnus and zebras, by the hundreds. The rangers, who accompanied us, took the cars to where large herds of gazelles, waterbuck, and gnus could be seen at close quarters. We also saw more ostriches, monkeys of different species, and an amazing variety of water fowls and cranes. But, our minds were set on seeing the monarch of them all, the Simba, the Lion. The rangers spotted a male sitting on a mound, sunk in waist deep grass; the cars proceeded towards him; the animal looked on with royal unconcern. But, as we moved near, we very nearly ran over two lionesses that were having their siesta amidst the grass. Luckily, they rose in time and moved deliberately off. We negotiated the rovers all around the beasts, within a few yards off where they lay. We were surprised at their timeless, forgetting that they have all the wild mischief unimpaired in their sinews. They are accustomed to cars and the movement of vehicles, but not to human beings. We left the lions with a pang, for we had begun to like them. They seemed so gentle and they appeared to like being looked at. Soon, we saw a lioness, with magnificent gait like a Dowager Queen, walking on what appeared to be a constitutional. Evidently, she was on a more deadly mission, for we could see buffalo and gnu alerted mysteriously and disappearing into the distance. Baba told us that the giraffes must have acted as walking observation posts and communicated by some secret sign the news of the approaching enemy. Baba was more interested in the process of mutual co-operation and mutual service, than in the strategy of terror and of the death.

At 4 p.m., Baba left the crater by plane, but not before He blessed the rangers with signs of grace. Since they could not grasp the supreme value of *vibhuti*, Baba created for them by a wave of the hand, pictures of Himself, which He knew they would treasure as mementoes of the happy hours spent in His company, and gave one to each of them. For the Britisher, who was the pilot of His plane, Baba created a charming portrait of Christ, with the Sacred Heart. He must have wished for a portrait of Baba, when he saw the rangers getting it - for, Baba asked him, "Do you want My picture, too?" and when he nodded, the wave of the hand created one for him, too.

Our single engined Super Wagon followed, soon. She did a splendid job, however, after the inevitable bumps while over the surrounding ranges; near Lake Natron, there was a newly formed volcano, a perfect cone of hot ash thrown up from the bowels of the earth, about 8000 feet above the sea level; the aircraft climbed over it and gave us the never-to-be-forgotten peep into the very mouth, from which we could see the wisps of smoke rising up, as incense to the God of Fire. We had to hover around for some ten minutes over the Nairobi National Park, casting glances at giraffes and ostriches, before we were allowed to land at Embaksi Airport.

Nairobi was all astir, for Baba was to address a public gathering in the city that evening at 6-30. The roads that led to the place of meeting were jammed with cars and men. The rush was unprecedented in the history of that city, for no spiritual leader had such universal appeal as Baba, who had no specific sect or creed or church, but who built His shrine in every heart with Love as the cement and faith as the brick. There must have been at least 20,000 people present, to have His *darshan* and to listen to His words. When He came into the grounds, Baba sensed the yearning that the men and women, sitting since hours, had in their innermost hearts. Instead of moving towards the brightly illumined dais, He turned His steps among the people. They made lanes for Him to pass; many touched His feet, others gazed at His face and drank deep the grace It bestowed; every one had the great chance of *darshan* at very close quarters. When at last He ascended the dais, all eyes were fixed on Him, all hearts were tuned to hear His discourse.

Baba started His discourse with the word of address, *"Divya-Atma-swarup"*, that is to say, He addressed the vast gathering as "embodiments of divine *Atma*". Each one before Him was, for Him, a spark of the divine fire, a wave of the vast ocean of divinity. In fact, this was the message of Baba, in Africa as well as elsewhere. He sees and advises us to see, behind the skin, the physical encasement, the habitation of flesh and blood, the One Indivisible All - forming God. This vision is the surest means and the strongest basis for love, among all beings. The discourse of Baba was devoted to the elaboration of this theme, which was specially valuable in the context of East Africa. Dr. C. G. Patel had referred in his introductory speech to the mental agitations of Indians in that continent, and Baba's message of love, built on the recognition of identity, was the *upadesh*, the spiritual panacea.

Baba prescribed the recitation of the name of God, the word that is transmuted into flesh; the call that is answered by the Loving Lord, the name that is the summary of the attributes and glory of God. He Himself sang a few of these rosaries of names, *Nama-mala*, thrilling the thousands with the honey melodiousness of His Voice and the meaningful variety of the attributes, described by the names.

Returning to His residence in the city, Baba sat before the television set, a medium of communication which some members of His party were seeing for the first time. The pictures that were projected led to a discussion on the harm done by that popular means of entertainment. Baba said that such powerful media should not be used for *Tamasic* and *Rajasic* purposes (deadening the higher emotions and arousing the lower passions). They should be turned into instruments for awakening the *Satwic* tendencies latent in man, tendencies which prompt him to revere the aged, the pious, the wise, to look upon all manifestations of goodness and greatness with awe, to be humble and simple, to be the master of one's passions and prejudices. "Since the aim of the sponsors of these programmes is to bring more and more people before the sets and make them watch with interest, tastes are vulgarised to suit the animal nature of man which revels in crime, violence, and viciousness. If the sponsors are taught to revere man as embodiment of divinity, they will not degrade him and defame him, as fit only for such vulgar fare," Baba said. He characterised the *Tamasic* and *Rajasic* items broadcast in television as *'televisham'* (tele-poison; *visham* in Sanskrit means, poison)! Baba is a relentless critic of films and books, and 'comics' that sow the seeds of sensualism and irreverence, greed and bloodthirstiness. From His boyhood, He campaigned against the appalling lowering of literary and artistic standards in the name of 'popular appeal'.

Nairobi is the only city in the world, where people are awakened by the roar of wild lions. The suburbs are occasionally visited by the lions, who lived here until a few years ago. In fact, the Nairobi National Park can be called its suburb inhabited by animals, zebra, gazelle, gnu, giraffe, impala, cheetah, leopard, and the lion, with attendant hyena. "You are quite likely to find lions lolling on the road," a friend told us; we found cheetahs, five of them engaged in an intimate conference in the centre of the road. They felt our cars unwelcome intruders and slowly adjourned to a place beyond the road, uttering unspeakable curses on us for interrupting their deliberations. We went to the hippo pool and discovered a big 'school' of them in a stream, infested by crocodiles. Baba spoke of the co-existence of these two, as another example of co-operation in nature. When we returned from the pool, we were rewarded by the majestic sight of two magnificently maned lions, lying nuzzling each other, on a flat piece of high rock. As our three cars neared them as close as ten feet, they rolled over in leisurely indolence and posed like film stars among fans for shots from a dozen cameras. Then, they walked towards the harem, a little distance away, where three lionesses, each a lithe, well-groomed, wiry beauty, were having their afternoon siesta. We left them on the rocks and came away, reluctantly to the city of Jacaranda and bougainvillea.

After lunch, Dr. Patel took Baba and the party in cars, to Nanyuki, 6400 feet above sea level, lying right on the Equator. The place is 123 miles from Nairobi; it is the place from where the climb to Mount Kenya (17,000 feet) is undertaken. The fine, tarmac road twists and climbs over the ridge, through coffee and sisal estates, with the round thatched huts of the traditional Kikuyu on open grounds. Up in the forest, redolent with equatorial density of green, is the Secret Valley, where Baba's party spent the night, watching leopards and other game, for a little while and filling themselves with the wisdom imparted by the Master. The much advertised leopards came almost on time, a mother and two cubs, and leaped up to the platforms where food was kept for them, undisturbed by the click of cameras and the flood light that was put on, for the sake of the onlookers of the banquet. But, Baba was not interested in them. He said it was a pity that He and they were in the thick of the jungle, far away from the hundreds of devotees at Nairobi, who would have been delighted to spend the Thursday evening hours in *bhajan*, in His Presence. Baba felt that they could spend the time to better advantage, if He could answer the questions that members of the Party might desire to put to Him. The questions were about the mind and its control and Baba described how the mind gets coloured by the objects it dwells upon. He contrasted the fly, which indiscriminately sits on fair and foul and the bee, which seeks to gather only honey. While illustrating by a wide gesture of the hand, Baba produced from His open palm, a big locket, of enamelled gold, with His portrait on it. We had scarce recovered from the amazement, when He placed it in the hands of a devotee, sitting before Him, saying, "Here, wear it; you have been wishing for this for long." Then, He turned to the rest of us and said, "That was for only one of you; perhaps, you want, each of you, something, this Thursday, in this Secret Valley." He waved the Hand and lo, there was a vase in His palm, with a screw top. It was full to the brim, with *Amrita*, sweet beyond words, fragrant beyond imagination. 11,000 feet above the sea level, on that cold night in Secret Valley, Thursday night, *Guruvar*, the day when the Master is to be adored, that Hand gave us through that golden spoon, the *Amrita* from that golden vase... that was indeed the expression of His spontaneous grace. Years of prayer and penitence might not earn it. It was like rain from a clear, blue sky, an act of Providence, pitying the drying crops on Earth!

The owner of the lodge, a Muslim, was called in and when Baba told him of the enlarged tonsils he was suffering from and gave him the curative *vibhuti* created for him, on the spot, he said, "I am indeed blessed." He got from Baba a portrait of His, which He created for him. The servants were not ignored; they got the coveted few minutes with Baba and the comforting counsel He confers on all.

Back at Nanyuki, Baba was approached by a group of people, who had come some distance from the interior, hoping to meet Him and crave His grace on a half-blind boy. Baba asked that he be brought to Nairobi, where He would stay until they came. And He called them in, when they came. I saw the father in tears, when the party came out from the room. They were tears of joy.

Baba drove to the Wilson Airport, Nairobi, to board the chartered plane and fly to Kampala. He was welcomed there by about a thousand devotees engaged in *bhajan*. They rose and rushed forward to touch His Feet, but Baba advised them to keep within the barricades, for, "Sai devotees should set a good example to all; they should not break rules intended to ensure the safety and comfort of all." The aircraft took us over the Rift Valley and the Highlands of Kenya, covered with charming plantations of tea and coffee. Kisumu, the harbour town, on the edge of Lake Victoria, was sighted and after a short dash across the Lake, we reached Entebbe and had a comfortable landing.

5.

Right Into The Heart

Baba had spent fifty hours away from Kampala; the thousands, who had tasted His compassion and His grace, could not bear that long separation. They prayed that He must stay on. That evening, when Baba moved among the gatherings during *bhajan*, letters were handed to Him, hundreds of them, pointing out the pangs that separation had caused. "Father, do not leave us" - was the theme. When Baba left India, the proposal was that He would leave East Africa on the 10th of July. The 10th was the "Guru Pournima", the holy day, the Full Moon Day, set apart in the Hindu calendar for the worship of the spiritual Preceptor, who directs the aspirant towards the *goal*, the *guru*. Baba was both *guru* and *goal*. Moreover, the "Guru Pournima" Day is associated in the minds of all devotees with a 'Miracle of Miracles' six years ago, when Baba saved a great devotee, by taking on Himself the fatal, paralytic stroke that he was about to suffer from! But, the prayers of Kampala were heard and India was informed by cable, that the return was postponed.

Someone said that the Sai family now included many Africans and so, this pournima will be in the midst of the new Sai family itself. Baba reacted to this remark in His characteristic manner, "Do not tell Me of a new Sai family; I am *Sanathana* (Ancient, Eternal) come as *Nutana* (New). Shall I tell you who the constituents of the Sai family are? The family of every Sai devotee? His father, *Truth*; his mother, *Love*; his wife or her husband, *Detachment*; his son, *Wisdom*; his daughter, *Fortitude*; his kith and kin, the *Good*; his friends and companions, the *sages* and *saints* - such is the Sai family. You speak of the Sai family, believing yourselves to be Sai devotees. But, it is not enough if you label yourselves as 'devotees'. I must accept you, as such. And I will accept, only when you act up to the teachings I give. And they are not difficult either. Be true, be just, be full of love, remain unaffected by the ups and downs of life. Take everything as signs of grace."

The High Commissioner for India, in Uganda, Shri. K. P. R. Singh called on Baba that evening and had a long conversation with Him. Later, about a hundred inquiries, mostly Headmasters of schools in Kampala, advocates, rotarians, and 'Lions' gathered at Dr. Patel's bungalow and Baba came them and, pushing aside the chair that was placed for Him, He sat with a charming smile, on the floor in front of the group. There was silence for a few minutes. It was broken by Baba's loving question, "Come on! Ask Me any question."

And, the questions that came from them! But, Baba is Love itself. He tolerated even very intimate, personal ones and replied with His natural sweetness. The first one was about Sai Baba being a Muslim, the second one about the 'miracles'. Baba declared that the 'miracles' were 'natural' to Him. "There are two types of happenings, which you refer to as miracles. One type goes against nature and her laws. They are the result of arduous, ascetic, yogic practices and are not beneficial to oneself or others. The other is the spontaneous manifestation of divine power and they lead men towards the divine," Baba replied. Others followed and Baba was engaged in answering them for more than an hour. Finally, a rotarian asked for a message, which all can carry with them in their hearts. Baba said, "Work is Worship, Duty is God, have this as the prime motive in all that you do." Then, He rose and moved among the members, creating *vibhuti* for those, whom He blessed. To the followers of Christ, He created portraits in enamel gold of Christ; to Muslims, He created, when they wanted it, portraits of Himself; to a Sikh gentleman, He gave a portrait of Guru Nanak, produced in a trice by a wave of the Hand. It was all spontaneous, smooth, silent, divine, suffused with love and benediction! Baba allowed a cameraman to take a photograph of the group, with Himself in the centre.

Later, He granted an audience to the officers of the immigration department, Uganda. They had come to know, earlier than others, about the visit of Baba and so, pleaded with Dr. Patel that they should be given a chance to meet Him. Baba knew their yearning and He satisfied it. That evening, there were about 15,000 earnest persons at the *bhajan* and Baba moved along the paths in their midst, receiving the hundreds of 'notes' handed to Him, appealing to Him to extend His stay. There were also notes, like, "Father! Relieve me of my pain," "Father, I shall come with You. I wish to be trained by You for service of my fellowmen here."

On the 7th, during the morning *bhajan* sessions, Baba selected more than a hundred persons from the gathering for individual attention and cure. Most of them were Africans from the villages around. He was engaged with them, until nearly midday.

Baba does not need, nor does He take rest. So, after the group selected had dispersed, He was engaged in a discourse to a number of doctors, who were waiting. It was question hour again. To the question, "Why is there so much evil in the world?" Baba said, "There is no evil in the world; it is the mind that sees evil; the darkness has no independent existence; it is only the absence of light. The skin of the orange is bitter; the bitterness is to guard the sweetness of the orange from spilling over and to protect it from pilferage.

The thorn plant is for the sake, a fence around the crops."
Someone asked, "If there is God, why cannot we see Him?"
Pat came the answer, "Who are you? Have you discovered
your 'I'? And then, why should you 'see' Him? You are really
He, know that. God is the action and the reaction; the original
and the reflection; the gross and the subtle; the substance
and the shadow. Nature is but the vesture of God. It is Maya,
His own elusive manifestation. How then can you see it?
You have to turn your eyes inward, away from visible objects
to the 'seer' that enables you to see. It is a difficult process
with many steps, but each step renders the next one easier."

In reply to another question, He said that desire or
Trishna (Thirst) is the prime cause for misery and that if a
person examines his desires, he can easily find that he can
live much more comfortably with much less, that his home
is filled with unused or unusable lumber. "Look at things
with less attachment; try to live simple lives. Derive joy from
the spring of joy inside you, not the objects around you. If
you extend your love to all, no one will hate you or envy
you and so, you can have the peace you crave for," He
advised.

He referred to jealousy as the professional disease of
doctors and lawyers, and exhorted them to make every effort
to overcome it. "Be happy, when another person is happy
or earns a good reputation," He said.

"Feed the mind as you do the body; have a regular
breakfast of *Dhyana*, a lunch of *bhajan*, a tea of scriptural
reading, and a dinner of *Namasankeertan* or *namasmaran*," He
proposed. When the doctors asked for some advice
applicable for all, He laughed and said, "You are doctors;
you do not prescribe the same medicine, when four persons
come to you, complaining of stomach-ache, do you? You
give one person sodium bicarbonate and bismuth, another

salts, a third one a poultice, and the fourth, perhaps you operate upon immediately, for appendicitis. Well, I shall tell you of two things that you can take; *Sadhana* (Spiritual disciplines regularly undertaken) and *Vichara* (intellectual inquiry). The two are not opposed to each other; they are complementary, like insulin and dietary restrictions for the diabetics. And then, let Me tell you, you should honour the affirmations you pronounce, the oaths you solemnly take, when you take the medical degrees at the University Convocation. Alleviate suffering as much and as quickly as you can," Baba said.

That evening, Baba addressed the first public meeting of the citizens of Kampala at the spacious grounds of the Patidar Building, in the heart of the town. Though the meeting was announced for 6 p.m., the grounds were packed with people as early as 4 p.m. As far as the farthest fence, people sat in thick mass and the roads had cars all along the right and left, for long distances. Baba moved into the park, preceded by a plentiful cluster of enterprising cameramen. The dais was decorated with simple dignity and lit in subdued floodlight. Behind the chair for Baba, the emblem of His universality and integral divinity revolved slowly, when each section came on to view, the Om of Hinduism, the Cross of Christianity, the dharmachakra of Buddhism, the Crescent and Star symbolising Islam, and the Fire revered by the followers of Zoroaster, featuring the manifold aspects of the one Truth. But, Baba did not direct His steps towards the dais. While devotees, men and women, sang *bhajans*, Baba went along the passages between the men and the women, on His Mission of grace. Full twenty minutes, He walked among them, spreading joy all around Him.

Then, He ascended the dais and Dr. C. G. Patel offered the homage of grateful welcome, in a few appropriate sentences. Baba sang a poetic prologue to His discourse, an impromptu *shloka*, in Sanskrit, denoting that unalloyed devotion alone is capable of conferring the fullest liberation to man, from the bonds of grief and pain, greed and avarice, birth and death. Such devotion being but another name for sublime love, the discourse was mostly on love and its efficacy in solving the problems of the individual, society, and the world. He concluded the discourse with the most enchanting singing, in His sweet sovereign voice, of four exquisite *'Namavalis'*, on different forms and names of God.

Baba said later that He had to avoid reference to the stories of the Ramayana and the Mahabharata or to the Gita, in His discourse, because the gathering consisted of people of all religions. In India, these stories provide good illustrative material, for every one knows the chief characters and the design of plot and counterplot, which the epics weave around them. "Here, in Uganda, I emphasised the basic requisites for a good and contented life, a life without suffering or grief."

On the 8th July, Shri Madhvani, the Indian industrialist of Jinja came to Baba's residence and was able to have *darshan* and a long interview with Him. The minister for information and broadcasting, Hon'ble Ojira came later and had the opportunity of a long talk with Baba. He felt sad that he could not, for reasons of health, come to Baba as soon as He reached Kampala. The Ugandan Parliament was having its sittings at the time and so, many of his colleagues could not find the time to pay their respects to Baba. The ministers of Uganda were an earnest, efficient band of patriots, who were determined to put their motherland on the road to progress. Their efforts had made the land, within a decade of Independence, happy and clean, progressive and prosperous. The Minister of Defence, Hon'ble Onama had the pleasure of the interview with Baba on the same day.

The *bhajan* sessions in the morning (from 8 a.m. till 11 a.m.) was the golden chance every day for students, young men, and the villagers to draw unto themselves the grace of Baba, to relieve their pain or activate their hopes. Baba slowly walked in front of the farthest line of anxiety, to pick the persons whom He planned to cure, console, or correct that day. As days passed and the news of the unique chance spread along the wires and roads, the mass of humanity became denser and denser, but Baba was rendered only happier, when He saw the numbers standing or squatting over the wide plains and the broad roads.

That evening too, there was a public meeting. At the Patidar's building area, there was a huge gathering. Baba arrived a few minutes earlier and moved among the people longer, in order to calm their hearts and prepare their minds for the message that was to be given. The *bhajan* songs were exhilarating, providing the sanctity backdrop for Baba's shower of grace. Then, when Baba spoke, it appeared as if the door of heaven had opened; the symphony of the divine angels adoring the Almighty arose in the hearts of the thousands, when Baba, through His thematic song, called upon all tongues to taste the nectarine sweetness of the name of God. The name, any name; the name capable of projecting on the mind the vast potential of divine might; this, Baba advised everyone to keep on the tongue and treasure in the heart, "Let It be your constant companion, as the staff of life, as the breath of the nostrils, as the unceasing thud of the heart," He said. It was a discourse that appealed to the innermost yearnings of all.

Returning to His residence, Baba saw Himself on the television set, for the broadcast was on, with pictures of the Defence Minister and the Information Minister having the interview with Him in Dr. Patel's Bungalow. The announcer had grasped the significance of Baba's visit and the vital essence of His message, for he said, "Yesterday and today, He addressed huge gatherings at Kampala. At both meetings, He emphasised the need for brotherliness and love, between all countries and creeds." After dinner, Baba saw a short film, depicting the Wild Life of Africa - lions, herds of elephants, rhinos, and crocodiles.

On the 9th of July, after the *bhajan* in the morning, Baba met members of delegations from Nairobi, Jinja, Mbale, Tororo, Nakuru, Eldoret, and a few other towns in Uganda and Kenya, since they were desirous of canalising the enthusiasm and devotion sown by His visit into constructive institutions, which will translate them into action. The ideal of service as Sadhana was explained by Baba to them:

"*Karmayoga* is for the attainment of purity of mind, escape from egoism, and the removal of the fog of ignorance from the firmament of the heart," He said. At last, it was decided to have Sathya Sai Seva Samitis in Uganda, Kenya, and Tanzania, in the first instance, in Africa. The headquarters was to be in Kampala. The Samitis of Kenya and Tanzania were to have Vice-Chairmen, wokring under the general guidance of the Uganda Unit. Baba laid down certain general lines of Sai service - free medical help by doctors, free legal aid by lawyers, *bhajan* classes, study circles, helping illiterate men and women in distress, visits to hospital wards, etc. He wanted that social work among Africans must be intensified and must be filled with love and care. The delegates had the privilege of securing the chance of a group photograph with Baba in their midst.

In the afternoon, Baba met a large group of spiritual aspirants, who wanted clarification from Him, on many points of practical application. Some of their problems were too intimate and so, Baba had to grant them separate interviews. The more general questions were answered, patiently and with simple illustrative stories, and they returned wiser and more enlightened. The *bhajan* sessions compelled the members to disperse rather unwillingly. At 8 p.m., the Minister of Internal Affairs, Hon'ble Bataringay came for interview, because he had heard from other ministers, who had met Him earlier, that no one should miss the chance of contacting the master, who had come from the East. After the interview, he confessed he had a most revealing experience.

6.

The Teacher

The tenth of July was *Guru Pournima* Day, the Day when spiritual aspirants dedicate themselves anew at the Feet of the Master. *Guru* means 'spiritual preceptor' and every year, the full moon of this month is set apart for the adoration of one's own master as well as all teachers of spiritual discipline, down from the very first of them, the great Vyasa, who collated the Vedic hymns, wrote the popular epics and the great, classic treatise on Atmic science, named *Brahmasutra*. Baba is the *Guru* and guide to hundreds of thousands in India and abroad and so, His physical presence is much sought, on this day of all days. Baba had proposed that He would leave Kampala, at 10 a.m., on that day, after giving *darshan* to devotees there and flying across the Arabian Sea, land at Bombay by 9:45 p.m., so that devotees there, too, can get coveted chance before the day ends. It would have been hailed by both continents as a happy sharing of grace. Baba decided to give the entire day to the African people, giving other places only signs and indications of His presence. Special banners spanned the roads along which all Kampala poured into the *bhajan* pandal that morning. With Jitu, the Tanzanian singer, the group of choirists gathered around the portrait of Baba and started their adoration, at dawn. Baba graciously received the homage of Dr. Patel and the member of his family, as well as of the devotees who had come with Him from India, and proceeded to the vast sea of expectant faces, awaiting to bloom at His appearance. The Africans fell on their knees as He approached them and offered roses and lilies, in lovely bouquets. The Indians took the dust from where His feet had pressed the ground and placed it on their heads. It was a most moving sight and I could not restrain the tears of joy that welled in my eyes, that I could see and get inspired by this sincere, spontaneous devotion to my Lord, who had declared, "I am all the Gods that every man adores."

It took nearly two hours for Baba to give *darshan*; Baba went far into the nooks and corners, seeking out those who were in the sun, so that they might return quicker home. He gave everyone *vibhuti*, the traditional sign of the *Guru's* grace, and nectarine *prasad*, indicative of the sweet and loving temperament that one must cultivate for one's own liberation. The Uganda Argus (English Daily) featured an article on Baba that day, with a number of photographs depicting His activities in that country. It said, "Sri Sathya Sai Baba maintains that the fundamental principles of all religions in the world are the same."

We were wondering whom Baba would bless with His *upadesh*, spiritual instruction, that day. Baba is the embodiment of Love and so, He chose the 'volunteers', the band of about 200 men and women, young and old, who were doing remarkably well, the service of controlling the people at the *bhajan* sessions and gatherings. The police of Uganda were a fine good-humoured lot of devoted men; from curiosity and wonder, they had turned into admiration and attachment; Baba shed special grace on them, especially, those who accompanied Him in the pilot cars and scooters.

But, the traffic regulation and security arrangements of the police were ably supplemented by this band of volunteers, who had no previous training for the job, nor any experience of such mammoth gatherings. Devotion to duty, reverence for their elders, steady disregard for personal comforts - these were their only equipments. After returning to India, Baba spoke at Bombay at the Reception

Meeting on 15th July, appreciating the work of the volunteers and gently chiding the Bombay Sathya Sai Seva Dal, for not having come up to the standards of the Uganda volunteers, though they have had many opportunities of service and many weeks of training.

When the men and women assembled at Dr. Patel's bungalow, Baba turned His eyes on them and surprised many by asking why a few, whom He mentioned by name, had not yet arrived. No one could guess that He knew the names of men and women engaged in this work, outside the bungalow, in the pandal and at the Patidar's building, or that He knows the names of all. He told them that He was talking to them that day, because they had deserved it. During the discourse, He called upon them to watch for chances to serve and be prepared by training and spiritual practices, to serve well.

Retiring into the bungalow, He continued the talk in the family circle of the Patels. "Men are like flint; it has latent heat; when it strikes against another flint, sparks emanate and they can be fed, until a big fire is caused. The second flint is usually some calamity or loss or disappointment. These sharpen the brain and reveal the Truth. Success and prosperity deadens the intellect and make intelligence blunt. Failure prompts inquiry, resulting in the struggle to remove the causes thereof. So, welcome failure as spurs to activity," He advised. He spoke about the details of *Namajapam* (the recitation of the name of the Lord) with a view to purify the mind. He considered the utility of rosaries and declared that they are helps, only for some preliminary period of time. "They distract attention, unless turning them round becomes automatic; then, they are no good at all. If rosaries render *japam* automatic, it is best to avoid them. Why keep a count of the number of times you call on God," He asked.

On the 11th, during *bhajan*, many of those, who received packets of *vibhuti* the previous day, announced with great joy that when they opened them at home, they found to their surprise and satisfaction that they contained not only the gift of grace that others got, but also small but clear portraits of Baba, which had been created therein by the unexpressed will of Baba Himself! They said they will cherish them as talismans, for He, who created them, must be able to guard them from harm. Another sign of Baba's divine power was revealed, when a doctor announced that his *ayah* (nurse-maid) had been granted an interview by Baba, along with others and that Baba spoke to her in the only language she knew, namely Swahili! In the evening, Baba sanctified the surgery of Dr. Patel in the city and blessed the compounder and other attendants with the *vibhuti* created on the spot, charged with mighty potentiality. From there, He drove to the houses of a few devotees, but though the visits were kept strictly confidential, people knew that He was coming and they hurried thither to get one more *darshan* of the charm, of which we can never have enough.

On the 12th, long before dawn, preparations were made for the drive to Murchison Falls National Park, and the party left at 6:30 a.m. in three cars. One of the party members did not turn up in time, since fever had intervened and laid the person low. But, Baba said, "Here! Take this *vibhuti*," and waved His hand. The *vibhuti* was taken, the person rose and dressed up quick, and became the most active member of the party, throughout the day! Baba's car sped along, quicker than the rest and when He reached Masindi (136 miles), the small town which is the stepping-off point for visits to the Park, He said, "One car has broken down," and later, when He reached the Park, about 50 miles away, He said, "They have hired another car at Masindi." Baba sees all and knows all. As the Gita describes God, *He* has *"hands and feet all over the Universe; He has eyes, head, and face, everywhere at all times."* As a matter of fact, the car had trouble at Nakasongola, 72 miles from Kampala; Baba was aware of it, the moment it happened; Baba became aware of the hiring of another car, the moment it was done at Masindi!

54 miles after Masindi, we entered the Murchison Falls National Park. At the very gate of the Park, the notice 'Elephants have the right of way' greeted us. Though happy that this promised us the sights of herds of elephants, which might be crossing the road, some of us were rather nervous, for we did not know how far we have to be from an elephant, which crosses the road, and how long we are to be delayed by these interruptions. There were some wild buffaloes at the gate, as an advance reception committee, and a scattering of deer and antelope on the grass 'downs'. We reached the Nile and crossed it in motor launches, sitting in our cars. On the other bank, around the Para Safari Lodge, when we motored to the Porch, we had to yield right of way to two huge tuskers and a cow-elephant, which chose to cut across. They appeared to be full of strength, serenity, and wisdom. We felt it was a misnomer to call them wild. But, we were told that there is a big gap between appearance and reality. So, we turned towards the cottage near the river's bank and there, joined Baba, graciously waiting for our cars, too, to join His.

Then, a motor boat was booked and we spent about three hours, in unforgettable experience, going up the fast, full Nile, gushing down in a wide, wild flood from the Falls above. The scene on both banks, far into the misty mountain ranges was a colourful kaleidoscope. The boat took us very near scores of 'hippo schools', where we could see those heavy, round monsters napping phlegmatically, below the water level, with eyes, nostrils, and ears protruding over the water! Hundreds of them, in huge patches of 'protrusions'!

Some rose; their thick necks and thicker heads popped fully over the water. Some were walking on the marshy bank, with their chubby kids trailing behind them. The red, mucus sweat on their bodies gave them a well-cooked appearance. Then, the crocodiles! Winston Churchill had seen them 60 years ago, in this same place; when he saw one of them basking in the sunshine on a large rock, with his mouth wide open and his fat and scaly flanks exposed, he fired a shot. "What the result of the shot was, I do not know. For, the crocodile gave one leap of mortal agony or surprise and disappeared in the waters. But then, it was my turn to be astonished... At the sound of the shot, the whole of this bank of the river, over the extent of at least a quarter of a mile, sprang into hideous life and my companion and I saw hundreds and hundreds of crocodiles of all sorts and sizes, rushing madly into the Nile. At least a thousand of these saurians had been disturbed by that single shot." Even now, there are thousands of these, drowsing on the bank, many about 20 feet long, with wide open, oral traps. It was a weird encampment of scaly horror. And the hippos were moving among them, huge rolls of flesh, but feeling safe and secure amidst the awful array of teeth. Herds of elephants were seen browsing 'elephant grass' on the plains above the river banks, where papyrus reeds grew in abundance. As a writer, whose basic, raw material is paper, I was fascinated to see the reed, which was held sacred by the Egyptians 4,000 years ago and from which they manufactured 'paper'! Binoculars and cameras were focussed on the hippos, crocos, and elephants without intermission, by the members of the party. It was like passing through a hair-raising fairy tale come alive. Returning to the cottage, the tour of the park was continued beyond the opposite bank, to the rocks overhanging the Murchison Falls. All along the route, the rolling plains were dotted with herds of elephants, with many magnificent tuskers among the bulls. We saw wild dog, hyenas, a few cheetahs, and lots of antelope and gazelle.

The Falls provided us an amazing experience of light and sound, fury and ferocity, beauty and terror. We could hear the loud, ominous hum miles ahead; the low, vigorous murmur transformed itself into a growl and then a roar, as we neared the Falls. The broad river, the Nile, hurries down a series of small cataracts in foam and fluttering whirls, down a continuous stairway of hardest rock; some distance above the falls, the rock walls that lead the flood contract suddenly, till they are not even ten yards apart; through this 'strangling portal' (says Churchill), as from the nozzle of a hose, the tremendous river is shot in one single jet, down an abyss of a hundred and sixty feet. It is overwhelming, fascinating picture for the eye; it is a deeply disturbing cascade of thunder on the ear! Big clouds of spray are embellished by the rainbow; swirling vortexes below attract flocks of kingfishers and strange birds of prey.

Carefully tracing the way along the rain-wetted road, the cars returned from the Falls, only to stop on a few more occasions, for elephants to cross the path. We came near a huge monster, who appeared even more formidable, when he spread out his triangular shaped ears and lifted his head to show us the brightly shining ivory that he had grown. He stood at the head of his herd, barely ten yards from the line of cars and when he was satisfied that we had admired him enough, he turned aside and moved majestically off, carrying his six tons of vegetable flesh along with him.

Reaching Masindi, about 9 p.m., Bhagawan proceeded to a village about 80 miles off, Kikonda, by name, where a group of devotees had built a *bhajan mandir* for His adoration, in true native style, round and thatched, simple and elegant, for themselves and the workers of their estate. Baba graciously took His seat in the *mandir* and, creating *vibhuti* as a sign of His compassion, He gave that panacea for physical, mental, and spiritual illnesses to the labourers in the estate, who were sitting in one section of the cottage, destined to be the prayer hall. They were overjoyed to find that the divine person, whom their employer adored, granted them first the coveted sign of His mercy. Baba left Kikonda and reached Kampala at 1 a.m. to find a gathering of hundreds, engaged in *bhajan* and hoping to get *darshan* of Baba, when the valedictory waving of lights takes place. Baba responded to their prayers and walked into their midst. He stood on the decorated dais for a while, in order to give *darshan* to all, while the light was waved. His compassion was so great that He could not disappoint those expectant devotees.

On the way from Kikonda to Kampala, Baba was speaking about the wisdom of the wild. He wrote about it to Dr. V. K. Gokak from Kampala and so, it would be better if I quote from that letter itself, "We went round places, where many varieties of wild life roamed freely. We spent one night on a treetop, in a hut of planks and wooden pillars and props. We saw lions, leopards, cheetahs, zebras, bisons, giraffe - in fact, all species of wild animals and game. If one observes all these wild animals living in close collaboration in these areas, one is filled with pity at the human species that has lost these qualities of mutual help and loving co-operation. These animals are friendly with each other; they drink from the same pool; they eat together; one species are comrades of another; we found representatives of what are called 'natural enemies' caressing each other. I felt that they were teaching man a lesson in social and spiritual behaviour. Divinity was evident, clear and pure, in every one of them. We returned to Kampala describing to each other their nature and characteristics, as well as the mutual co-operation that they exhibited."

Baba has said often that all animals, except man are still adhering to their *dharma*, their essential nature and purpose. The lion has not changed its spots. But, man, who is divine in nature, has changed from human to bestial levels of behaviour and has even fallen lower into the dark and sinister regions of the demon and the devil. While touring round the Parks, seeking places where we could spot the denizens, Baba showed us how no bird or beast has deviated from its *Swadharma* and adopted *Paradharma*, as man has so shamefully done. To be with Baba, the Great Teacher, while the panorama of the wilds was passing across the windows of the car, was indeed a rare chance to know the secret of evolution and progress, for man and beast.

Baba had graciously extended His stay at Kampala, responding to the prayers of the people. But, Africa was not willing to part with Him! The people hoped that by more prayers, more intense prayers, prayers by more people, He could be again persuaded to postpone His departure. Parties came by chartered plane from Mwanza in Tanzania, Dar-es-Salaam, Mombasa, and other far off towns, with prayers that He should visit their places, before leaving for India. It must have been hard for any individual to set aside the flood of sincerity and start as scheduled, but Baba stays everywhere, not merely at the place where His Physical Presence is experienceable; and He can console and convince those, who pray for His Presence by signs and substantial proofs. So, though the mayor of Kampala tried his best to persuade Him to postpone, Baba said He had to leave!

On the 13th, even before dawn, thousands had gathered at the spacious structure, outside Dr. Patel's bungalow, for the news that Baba will be leaving on the 14th morning had spread and everyone wanted to share in the ecstasy of *bhajan* and the sanctity of *darshan*. From Jinja, Mbale, Kakina, Mbarare, Masaka, Igaye, Kabale, and other villages, where the Sathya Sai Seva Samiti and its women's section had arranged some programmes, like *bhajan*, as well as from many other villages, where the advent of the Lord had spread, persons, who had in their hearts a gleam of God, hurried Kampala-ward and sough the coveted *darshan*.

From 8 a.m. to 10 a.m., Baba was engaged in walking along the lanes of men and women, showering His grace on all. He stood in the midst of groups that prayed for a photograph with Him and satisfied their wish. A party of about 25 university students were the first to benefit by this opportunity. They offered Baba lovely rose bouquets, they struggled to get positions next to Him or behind Him; some of them folded their palms in Indian style and knelt in adoration. It was a sight that brought tears of joy, that reminded us of Baba's declaration at Bombay, He would soon enfold land after land, in the embrace of His Universal Unifying Love. The exaltation we experienced at that moment was heightened when some of them wept, while Baba patted them caressingly on their backs. "When are you coming again?" they insisted, when they learnt that Baba had decided to go, next day. Even the police constables, who were deputed for duty at the place where Baba stayed, were heroically trying to curb their sorrow. My heart strings very nearly snapped; I broke into sobs at the sight of those hefty six-foot constables wiping tears, when they contemplated the inevitable vacuum in their eyes as soon as Baba emplaned.

The evening *bhajan* session was also very crowded and Baba gave the people even longer hours for *darshan*. Many among the sick had from His hands the rare gift of *vibhuti*, while not a few got a fond pat on the head or back, from the Hand that fashions the fate of millions.

7.

Came The 14th Day Of July

The East African Airlines Friendship plane was to take Baba and His party from Entebbe Airport to Nairobi, where the Air India Boeing will be awaiting His arrival. The plane was leave Entebbe at 11 a.m. and so, thousands from Kampala proceeded on cycles, scooters, cars, and omnibuses to the airport, 21 miles away, in order to win one more *darshan* of Baba, while He boarded the plane. This struck me as a measure of the depth of the yearning that Baba had planted in the heart of the people of Uganda. The National Crest of Uganda carries as its motto, "For God and My Country," revealing to all the responsiveness of the people to the call of the spirit and of the divine voice.

With the singing of the glory of God raised from a thousand throats, Indian and African, the roads reverberated in joy. People could scarce see the departing cars, for their eyes were too full of tears. Baba blessed the vast gathering with His *Abhayahasta* (Hands raised to assure that one need not fear, for one has His grace in ample measure). At the very last moment, even while He was boarding the car, a person asked for His autograph on a book (At The Lotus Feet), which he proposed to send to his sick daughter. Baba wrote on the first page of the book, the advice, "DO GOOD, BE GOOD, THINK GOOD," and signed, "With Blessings, Baba," before handing the book back to him! Indeed, He is Love, Love, Love... full and free!

Just before taking off, while the aircraft turned on the tarmac for the final spurt, it was discovered that a wheel was defective and so, all passengers were asked to alight, until the needed repairs were executed. This gave the Ugandans two hours more with Baba, hours which the people of Nairobi had joyously planned to profit by. In their airport, they had planned a public gathering similar to the one, which Baba addressed when He arrived. In the V.I.P. Hall of the Entebbe Airport, Baba spent the time, granting interviews to many, who sought it and talking to Bob Raymer of USA, who had come with Him from India on his way home, about His visit to his place.

The plane left Entebbe at 1 p.m. and reached Nairobi at 2:30 p.m. Thousands were perched on the terrace since 1 p.m., but since the Boeing was waiting with its passengers for a long time, Baba insisted on boarding the plane immediately. He waved His hand to the vast gathering acclaiming, "Jai, Jai," and entered the plane. Only the president of the Sathya Sai Seva Samiti, Nairobi and a few of the members were able to approach the plane, in time, to place a garland of flowers round His head and touch His feet. The plane flew along Somaliland and Ethiopia to the Red Sea and landed at Aden, at 5:15 p.m. (Kampala Time, which we still had on our watches), that is about 7:55 p.m. at Bombay, 1910 miles away. During the halt at Aden Airport, Baba and party stayed on in the plane itself. A sizeable batch of devotees from Aden ventured to present themselves inside the plane; when Baba received them with a smile, they got confidence and courage enough to touch His feet! Baba created *vibhuti* for all and blessed them. They had known of His being in that boeing, by sheer chance and they were happy beyond words, that they could reach a long-planned goal after such a short pilgrimage!

The hour of quiet also afforded a fortunate chance to the air hostesses and stewards and other members of the crew to receive from Baba signs of His grace. It transpired that one of them had heard Baba's discourse and another had visited at Bombay, a home where through Baba's grace, *vibhuti* is showering from the picture of Baba that they keep in their prayer room! Similar gifts of chance were enjoyed by some of the passengers, too. One of them implored Baba to bless him; he said, "I tried to draw Your attention on myself at Kampala, for some days, at the *bhajan* sessions; I could not; I am happy, I am now in the same plane! I crave Your blessings." And Baba did not deny the gift. Miles above the earth, he got them.

It was 12:45 p.m., when the plane landed at Santa Cruz, with the uniquely precious cargo it carried. Thousands were awaiting Baba, though the hour was late. The sky was rent with acclamation, while He drove to Dharmakshetra, in the company of the president of Sri Sathya Sai Prasanthi Vidwan Mahasabha and the President of Sri Sathya Sai Seva Samiti, Bombay. Devotees from all over India were elated that Baba had returned after a fortnight of incessant ministration and teaching, consoling and comforting their brothers and sisters across the sea.

On the 15th July, about 20,000 persons assembled at Dharmakshetra, to felicitate themselves on securing as their Lord, the *Avatar* of the age, the Embodiment of *Sathya, Dharma, Shanti*, and *Prema*, who had set out on His task of blessing all humanity. Dr. K. M. Munshi (Founder of the Bharatiya Vidya Bhavan, dedicated to the spread of the fundamental inspiration of Indian culture) presided over the meeting. He said, he was long feeling dejected that faith in religion and faith in God are fast declining and that these two props of civilisation will fail us soon. But, he was happy to find that Bhagawan Sri Sathya Sai Baba is achieving the moral and spiritual regeneration that we stand sorely in need! If India is to survive, it can be only through spiritual uplift. He said he was very happy that Baba has come to do this very task. "He will certainly make India live again as

India, and through this process, He will spread faith and religion in the world. I offer my obeisance and respects to Him," he said. He joined with all, congratulating East Africa on the great opportunity it had, for seeing Baba and listening to His divine discourses.

Baba, in the discourse He gave, spoke of the visit to East Africa, in some detail. He said, "For the Eternal Absolute, the *ParamAtma-tatwa*, the universe is the mansion; going from one continent to another is only the Master moving from one room to another in that spacious mansion. I am surprised that you treat this sojourn in an adjacent room, as if it was a shifting into a new house! I am not alien in any country; I am native to all parts of Earth," He said. He spoke of the enthusiastic response, which the Message of Love received from the people and popular leaders of Africa, ministers, officers, commoners, and others. The spread of the Indian religious doctrine of the essential divinity of all beings will remove all hatred and malice, for it is only when you are unaware of the identity that you fight and hate. Karna, in the Mahabharata, fought vengefully to destroy the Pandava brothers, not knowing that he was eldest of them all! When he came to know that he and they were brothers, born of the same womb, he was torn by unspeakable anguish! Hate thrives on the ignorance of this reality of brotherhood. My discourses and conversation had the effect of intensifying cordiality between the Africans and Indians. Africans joined in the *bhajan*; Africans occupied most of the space in the *bhajan* sessions; the Indians had to be content with marginal accommodation.

Of course, you must expect differences between the faith of one people and another! Religion has to satisfy the needs of the time and the temper and the facet of Truth that most appeals to a people. The fauna and the flora of one country are distinct from those of another. So too, it is foolish to expect that all men in all lands will adore the same name and form of God, in the same manner, for the same gains. You must respect the differences and recognise them as valid, so far as they do not smother the spark of unity.

This was what I told the races and creeds of Africa. *Eshwarasarva bhootanam;* God is in every being. All are kin, made kin by this common link. It was this truth, unity being seen as diversity through the glasses of 'individuality' and ego - that was propagated in East Africa. And, people relished it and prayed that it might regulate their daily lives.

Give love; you are loved in return. Every one requested me to give them a portrait of Mine. I created them on the spot and gave them to many. Dr. Patel, who was with Me when I gave it to some officers, like the Inspector-General of Police, the Chief of Staff of the Uganda forces, pleaded with them to keep the portrait safe and secure, but they chided him for that superfluous advice. "We value it more than anything else," they declared. Quite a few requested for directions for *dhyana* and a *mantra* to repeat and meditate upon. I satisfied that desire also, for it was genuine and rising from the heart.

At Nairobi as well as at Kampala, the enthusiasm of the people was overwhelmingly ecstatic. It caused great joy to those, who were with Me. It was inspiring, so inspiring that I was stopped in the most unlikely places, in the midst of jungles, by the side of airstrips where we landed in chartered planes, by persons who sought grace.

Africans, who were not acquainted with the meaning or pronunciation of the *bhajans*, sang them in chorus, drawn by the strong current of devotion. College students, who acted as volunteers, were very earnest to serve; they had no training, no experience of such mammoth gatherings; but, the innate good sense and humility of the Ugandans made their task easy. No one fell on My feet as I passed along and no one obstructed another, or deprived another of the chance of *darshan*. The volunteers and sevadal workers of Bombay have had weeks of training and I have spoken to them often of their duties and obligations; but, yet, I must say, the volunteers of Kampala have scored points over them in discipline and joyful, untired service.

The people, whom I met there and those, who heard My discourses and talks and have had a glimpse of the Reality, upon which these waves of joy and grief, of loss and gain, perpetually rise and fall; many of them told Me that the vision of the Indian sages alone can save the world and fill the heart of man with peace. The splendours of the genuine culture of India will spread, in this manner, from country to country, from continent to continent, in the days to come; that is My task."

Thus, Baba fed the lamp of love in all hearts. Three weeks after He left Uganda, a Muganda teacher writes to Prasanthi Nilayam, "Act as my Redeemer; deliver me from grief. I am writing, because I have heard of the many miracles, which You did here and one of my best friends, who was about to touch You here, directed me to pray to You." An aspirant from Mukono writes, "O Lord, give me the strength to forgive those, who harm me; make me forget the injury I receive from them." These are intimations of the transmutation of attitudes, impulses, and urges that a moment's sight of Baba, a touch, or a word can bring about in man!

May the light of His Love illumine our hearts, too and may the whole world shine with sublime effulgence.

Part II

Discourses Of Baba In East Africa

1.

With Palms Folded

Dr. Chotabhai G. Patel, President, Bhagawan Sri Sathya Sai Seva Samiti, Kampala, Uganda spoke first, at the public gathering at Nairobi, Kenya, on the fourth day of July, 1968 - the first public meeting, which Baba addressed in East Africa.

"Fellow-devotees! These days will be written in letters of gold in the spiritual history of the world, for Bhagawan has left India for the first time now, to regenerate the moral and spiritual values of life in the West, the West afflicted by materialistic progress and the advancement of science.

We in East Africa are really lucky and blessed that Bhagawan has chosen this land to communicate His Message, especially when Asians here need His guidance urgently to solve their problems, which are mental more than anything else.

Two months ago, the World Conference of Sri Sathya Sai Organisations was held in Bombay. 1200 delegates from all parts of the world attended and decisions were taken on furthering the activities of these organisations and on measures to carry the message of love and peace to people of all lands. The Conference was unique, that it was held in the Presence of Baba, the Incarnation of the Divine, the Avatar. I believe that the first impact of the Conference is happily to East Africa, to which our beloved Lord has come in His physical form.

There are some here, who have had *darshan* of Bhagawan Sri Sathya Sai Baba in India; thousands are having that chance only today. We are grateful to Baba for vouchsafing us this unique piece of good luck. To see Baba is to love Him, to listen to His advice, to follow it, and to save oneself. Baba says, "It is not enough, if you love Me; you should make certain that I love you." In other words, we have to start following His advice, obeying His commands, practising His Message.

And, what is His Message? "Man must achieve peace, amidst joy and grief, gain and loss, victory and defeat, and all the dualities, which are inevitable; this peace can be won through *Sathya, Dharma, Shanthi,* and *Prema.*" We pray that Baba bless us with His Message to us, of East Africa; tell us our duties, the lines of activity for the Sathya Sai Seva Samitis, by which they can promote the welfare of the human race.

Fellow-devotees! Blessed are those born in the Sai era. More blessed are those, who are present here, today, in the immediate presence of the Lord and who will be able to have His *darshan* in the days to come, at Kampala and other places in East Africa. Let us fold our palms in prayer, that He may shower His choicest blessings on this land and make us worthy of His Love.

2.

The Message I Bring

(Discourse at Public Meeting, Nairobi, 4th July, 1968)

O ye, whose real Reality is the Divine *Atma*, remember that the one object of this human existence is to visualise that Reality, that *Atma*, which is your Truth. All other activities are trivial; you share them with birds and beasts; but, this is the unique privilege of man. Man has climbed up through all the levels of animality in order to achieve this high destiny. The years between birth and death are wasted in seeking food and shelter, comfort and pleasure as animals do. He is condemning himself as a fool. Man is endowed by the Creator with two special gifts; *Viveka* and *Vignyana* (the faculty of reasoning and the faculty of analysis and synthesis). He should use these gifts for discovering the Truth about himself, instead of frittering them in the pursuit of hypotheses about the world that hold good only for a while. All countries are borne and are sustained by this one world. All 'bodies' are inspired by the same divine principle, moved by the same divine motivator. The Vedas, which are the most ancient scriptural texts, declare, *"God is Sarvabhootantaraatma* (God is the inner Reality of all Beings). *Ishavaasyamidam Sarvam* (All this is enveloped in God). *Vasudevassarvamidam* (All this is God, Vasudeva)."

The divine principle or *Atma* that is in every one of you, equal and enlightening, is like the electric current that illumines the bulbs before Me, of different colours and different candle-powers; the same God shines in everyone, whatever be his creed or colours, nationality or faith. The current animates and activates all bulbs; the divine animates and activates all. Those, who see difference are deluded; they are befogged by prejudice or egoism or hatred or malice. Love sees all as one divine family.

Now, I have here a garland of flowers. It is made of hundreds of flowers, of different hues and fragrances, but though of many colours, many names, grown on many plants in many places, spreading many fragrances, they are all strung together on one thread - a thread that sustains them all, that runs through them all. That inter-penetrating string is the *Atma*, the divine, the *Brahmam*. The manifold world, the objective world, is the "Flower-aspect" of the garland; God is the "string" aspect.

How does the *Atma*-principle express itself in man? As *Prema*, as Love. This is the reason why Love is the basic nature of man, the quality that sustains the world and moves man onwards. Without Love, man will be blind; the world will be a dark and fearsome jungle. Love is the light that guides the feet of man in the wilderness. But, to get that light, there must be the current, the wire, and the bulb; *Sathya* or Truth is the current; *Dharma* or Righteousness is the wire; *Shanthi* or Equanimity is the bulb. It is only when these qualifications are gained, these supports are provided, that Love is rendered sublime; otherwise, it degrades and turns man into a heartless ogre. The Vedas laid down four goals before man, *Dharma, Artha, Kama,* and *Moksha* - all these goals are attainable, through the practice of *Prema*, or Love regulated by Truth, Righteousness, and Equanimity. But, man has got himself too involved in the entanglements of sensual pleasures to earn these virtues. He has neglected the goal of *Dharma* or Righeousness, which is the head and the goal of *Moksha* or Liberation from the chain of birth and death, which is the *Feet* of the Corpus of the *Purusharthas*. He is now caught in the meshes of *Artha* and *Kama* - the headless, feetless, lifeless corpse. The high teaching of the

Vedas is that man must earn *Artha* or wealth through *Dharma* or Righteousness; that is forgotten. Wealth is accumulated, anyhow. The Vedas taught that man should have only one *Kama* (desire), viz. *Moksha* or Liberation, for a prisoner can have no other desire than freedom from bondage. But, man is helplessly drowning himself in empty desires that never satisfy his deeper thirsts. All the present unrest, anxiety, and fear are due to this mistaken course.

The human body, with all its skills and potentialities, is a valuable gift granted by God. It has to be used as a raft to cross the ocean of *Samsara* (the flow of change and birth, growth, decline, and death), that lies between bondage and liberation. Awaken to this primal duty, early enough, even when your physical and mental faculties are keen, even when your power of discrimination is sharp. Do not postpone the voyage, for the raft might lose its capacity to float; the boat might spring a few leaks. The body might be burdened with illness, which clamours for attention. Think of the supreme joy you can derive, when you approach the shore of Liberation and resolve to launch the boat and move on. The joy that one derives through the senses, which cater to the body, is infinitesimal, when compared to it. Ride on the waters of *Samsara*, safe. No harm can come to you, even if the boat is for years and years on the waters. But, danger will engulf you, once the waters get into the boat! Be in *Samsara*, but let not *Samsara* get into you. That is to say, avoid attachments, be but a witness, do not crave for the fruit of any act of yours, take praise or blame, loss or gain, grief or pain with equal grace. Float, do not sink. The sensory pleasures are trivial; they are not worth worrying over. Pursue nobler ends, grander ideals. The sages have discovered the disciplines that will keep you unaffected and unattached; learn them. Practise them and earn unruffled Peace. The body can be compared to a cart. The horse that drags the cart is the mind. Paying more attention to the upkeep of the body is like putting the cart before the horse. Without mental balance, equanimity, and peace, one cannot have even physical health. The mind binds; the mind loosens the bonds. *"Mana eva manushyanam karanam bandha mokshayoh."* Therefore, I would advise you to pay special attention to the training of the mind.

The body might be reclining on a plush sofa in air-conditioned room, but if the mind is not trained to be at peace, but is agitated by imaginary fears, anxieties, and greed, the 'coolness' can only be skin deep. In homes and schools, the training of the minds of the young has to be taken up by the elders, who must themselves be equipped for this task, by steady practice, in meditation, recital of the name of God, silence, etc.

In every home, a certain length of time must be fixed every day, both morning and evening, for higher thinking, spiritual readings, singing the glory of God, reciting the names of God, etc. Really speaking, one should dedicate all one's lifetime to God, every thought, word, and deed to God; so, as a first step, a few minutes have to be devoted to His adoration and gradually, when the sweetness of the atmosphere heartens you and persuades you to devote more and more time, you will yourself do so. Remember, living is of achieving life in God. You are all entitled to that consummation. You can all one day become aware of the Truth and experience It, for you are the Truth. Do not lose faith. Do not belittle yourselves. You are divine, though you appear human and often slide down into animality and even worse.

Develop Love, share that love with all. How can you differentiate between one person and another, and treat them differently, when they are both of the same divine essence?

Forget the basic divinity, hatred sprouts; envy raises its head. See the same *Atma* in all and love. It is your love, your own *Atma*.

O ye *Premaswarupas*, Embodiments of Love, you have been sitting here in the open, under difficult conditions, for hours awaiting this chance of seeing and hearing Me; I speak so much, only to satisfy your ardour. For, when I sense your *Prema*, I feel like sharing it and allowing you to share My *Prema*, without the mediation of words. I have come to you only to light the lamp of Love in your hearts, to see that it shines with increasing lustre. I have not come to speak in support of any particular *Dharma*, like the Hindu *Dharma*, or on any mission of publicity for any sect or creed, or to attract disciples and devotees into My fold or accumulate followers for any doctrine. I have come to tell you of this unitary faith, this Atmic principle, this Universal Love, this all-embracing divine essence, this *Dharma* of *Prema*, this Obligation of love.

All *dharmas* and religions teach one basic discipline: *Chitta Shuddhi*, the cleansing of the mind, the removal of the blemish of littleness and egoism from the mind. Every religion teaches man how to fill his mind with the glory of God and remove therefrom the pettiness of conceit. It lays emphasis on detachment and discrimination, to teach man to reach the higher path towards liberation from bondage.

I want you to believe that all hearts are motivated by the one God, that all faiths glorify the one God, and that all names and all forms denote only that same God, whose adoration is best done by means of love. Cultivate that *Eka-bhava*, attitude of one-ness, of non-distinction, between men of all creeds, all countries, all continents. That is the message of love I bring. That is the message I wish you to take to heart.

Foster love, live in love, spread love - that is the spiritual exercise, which will yield the highest dividends. To make love grow with deep roots and wide-spreading branches sheltering the friendly and the unfriendly, you must take up another discipline, namely reciting the name of God, remembering His majesty and His glory, His grace and His might. He has a million names; the sages and saints of all lands have seen Him in a million forms; they have extolled Him in all the languages of the world, but yet, His glory is not exhausted by their description. Select any name of His, the name that appeals to you most, select any form of His, the form that appeals to you most. Every day, when you awaken to the duties of the day, recite the name, meditate on the form; have the name and the form as your companion and inspiration, guide and guardian throughout the toils of the day. When you retire at night, offer grateful homage to God in that form and with that name for being with you, by you, beside you, before you, behind you, all day long, doing thus, you will grow purer and stronger, every moment; you will not falter or fail.

I must give you one more advice. Endeavour always to promote the joy of your fellow-countrymen in this continent and endeavour also to share in that joy. Bharata is so called, because the people there have *rati* or devotion to *bha* or Bhagawan or God. They are devoted to God and all the children of God. They are afraid of sin; they are eager to acquire *gnyana*. So, I am happy to give this message to you; "Resolve upon the quest of your own Reality. Resolve to remember the name of God and to live in the inspiration of that remembrance. Cultivate love and share love with all."

I bless that you achieve success in this endeavour and derive great joy therefrom.

3.

The Medicine Needed

(Questions & Answers at the Gathering of Rotarians, Lions, Lawyers & Doctors on 6th July, 1968)

Swamiji, Shiva is said to be the greatest of the Hindu Gods; how then did He incarnate as Sai Baba of Shirdi, who was a Muslim?

Your statements are all incorrect. Shiva is only a name of God, like any other. There is no great, greater, greatest among these names. No name is all-comprehensive. Each signifies some aspect of divinity, some facet of the splendour, that has no limits. Again, Sai Baba was not a Muslim. He was a *Brahmin* by birth, of the *Apastamba Sutra* and the *Bharadwaja Gotra*. The name, Sai Baba, probably misled you. Sai means Sahi, Shahi, Lord, master, Prabhu; Baba means father; that is all. And how can limits be placed on God and His will to incarnate? One's experience alone is the best proof in spiritual matters; hearsay is of no value. Even experience is valid only as far as it goes. Each one conceives of God as he has experienced Him as having a form. Seven blind men approached an elephant and each understands it according to his own individual experience. One touches the leg and knows the elephant to be a pillar; a second contacts the tail, is sure it is a thick rope-like thing. A third, who handled the ear, swore that the elephant was 'a winnowing basket', while the fourth, who leaned against the stomach, argued that it was a wall. No one had a total experience; no one knew the entire animal. The entire animal is not even the sum total of all the individual experiences! When the sum total is known, a world religion will emerge.

Hinduism, Islam, Christianity, Buddhism, Zoroastrianism - are all partial expressions of that total Truth. Hinduism can be said to be stomach of the elephant, for through its principles, it can send sustenance to all the limbs, all the senses, and the brain.

Is a World Religion possible, Swamiji?

It is possible. When man discovers that the One Divine Principle activates all beings, as the same electric current activates all bulbs, fans, stoves, and machines that are driven by that power, then the world religion will be born. The recognition of this ever-present, universal, unseen activator, the immanent principle, God, will plant in each heart the spark of Love. In fact, it is there already. But, it is smothered by the force of 'mine' and 'thine', of greed and selfishness. All are waves of the same Ocean - that is the inspiration of world religion. That is the Truth, of which all religions are facets.

Swami, we know that greed and egoism are bad, that love alone confers Ananda; but, we find it difficult to act up to our convictions. Our case is like the person, who said, "Janami dharmam, na cha me pravritti; janamyadharmam na cha me nivritti."

That shows that your conviction is not strong, is not steady; otherwise, why should you feel like that person, "I know what is right, but I am unable to do the right; I know what is wrong, but I am powerless to desist from doing it." You are not quite convinced that a certain act is right; you are not quite sure that another act is wrong. You are talking without fixed faith. If you know for certain that the thing before you is a snake, you will not take a single step towards it, even if ten persons push you towards it, will you? Why do you commit a wrong, when as you say you know it is wrong? It is because, you are not quite convinced that it is wrong and fraught with dangerous consequences for you, if not now, at least later. Develop faith; make it strong and steady; be in the company of the good and the pious and the virtuous.

Swami, the scriptures, especially the Bhagavad Gita, extol Bhakti and Gnyana as paths to God realisation. They do not attach much importance to Karma; what is the value of Karma or Work in the spiritual field?

The Gita extols *Karma*, too. Work-Worship-Wisdom: that is the order; *Karma, Bhakti, Gnyana. Gnyana* is the last stage, the Stage of fruition, of fulfilment: *'Gnyanadevatu Kaivalyam'*, 'By *Gnyana* alone, Liberation is attained.' *Karma* is the flower. When it is preserved from falling off, when it is fostered and protected from pests, the fruit appears from it; that is *Bhakti*, the attitude of worship, of dedication, of surrender. Protect this tender fruit-thing, guard it and tend it, feed it and fend it, and you get the ripe fruit full of sweet sustaining juice of *Ananda*, the fruit of *Gnyana*. The three are not separate and several. It is a continuous process of spiritual discipline, the end-product being the realisation of Reality.

Swamiji, you are performing miracles. What is the purpose? Is it good for the people to know that the laws of nature can be broken?

No, no, I do not perform miracles. Of course, there are some, who perform feats; they have acquired some powers through *yoga* and they go about displaying them, in order to collect money or influence or followers or reputation; they indulge in *pradarshana* or exhibition. What you call miracles are just spontaneous evidences of My Divinity; I have not acquired the power to perform them, nor do I exhibit them for demonstrating My divinity. In fact, so far as you and I are concerned, "miracles' are not important at all. Pay more attention to other things about Me. When a son comes home for the holidays and is about to leave for college, the mother prepares a big feast with all the nice dishes he likes most. She does so out of sheer love, not to draw the son nearer to herself, or to impress upon him her talent in the culinary art. Her love is reflected back from the son as love. I too express My love and that expression is a *nidarshana* or evidence of divine power, which induces you to take to the Godward path. I do not set about to 'perform' what you call 'miracles'; it is My nature. It is My way of doing things, My way of expressing My love and grace.

Excuse me, Swamiji, for this question; if one has to suffer the consequences of Karma, whatever he has thought, spoken, and done, what is good of bhajan, Prayer, etc.?

As you say, one has to reap the consequences; every act, every thought, every word has its inevitable impact; but, from the previous life, only the impact of the major and the more powerful acts and *Karmas* are carried over to this life. The effects of every little *Karma* are not to be suffered from birth to birth. Besides, you must remember another point, which is encouraging. It is possible by means of repentance, contrition, and consistent good living to counteract the evil consequences. More than all, the grace of God is all-powerful. He can make the law of *Karma* ineffective, in your case; His grace can make the consequence of no consequence! The doctors among you know that certain drugs are dated; when that date elapses, the drug is ineffective, though it is to all appearance the same, unchanged in quantity, colour, or other characteristic. So too, the consequences of *Karma* may be in the bottle, but it can do no harm, it can produce no effect. Or, when a person is under morphine, the pain is there, but he is unaware of it. So, when the grace of God is won, the consequence of *Karma* might work itself out, but the person will be unaffected; so, it is as good as cancellation. *Karma* cannot harass you, when you are under the benign influence of divine grace. Illness can be cured and health can be restored, is it not? Similarly, the suffering due to past actions, thoughts, and words can be cured and equanimity restored.

What are the main principles of the Hindu faith, Swamiji?

One of the main principles is this: that each one is responsible for his own uplift or downfall, that he must reap what he sows, that he must himself win the grace of God to save himself from the suffering caused by ignorance. Then, the Hindu believes in the possibility and the authenticity of divine incarnations or *Avatars*, God assuming human form, in order to uphold truth and suppress falsehood. The Hindu also believes that God can be realised, visualised, here and now, through mental purification. When the mind is cleansed out of existence, One is all illumination, the splendour of the God that is his inner reality.

How can that be done, Swamiji?

The mind is like this handkerchief; warp and woof of yarn; the yarn is desires. Remove desires, conquer this tendency to satisfy them, and the mind is nullified. Desire leads to attachment, attachment soils the mind with hatred, envy, greed, lust, malice, etc. Every religion strives to teach methods of minimising desires and avoiding the pollution of the mind. *Chitta-shuddhi* (purification of the mind) is the aim, through the annihilation or sublimation of desire.

How can hatred and suspicion be removed from the mind, Swamiji? They are so deep-rooted in man.

Hatred and suspicion are signs of weakness. Become strong; then, there will be no need to hate or suspect! Only the timid are prone to hate. Hatred is a sign of egoism, of greed, of desiring something you do not deserve. Develop *vairagyam*, detachment; that will make you brave, free, full of courage. It will add strength into you.

Can non-violence win over all opposition, Swamiji?

Of course, it can. Only, you must have unshakable faith. You should not start compromising and discovering excuses for transgressing it.

But, Swamiji, people seem to have forgotten the apostle of non-violence so soon, even in his own country!

How do you know? Why do you worry over another's memory? If you feel that a certain line of behaviour is good, remember it yourself; that is the best you can do, to promote the cause you love. Why should you assume responsibility for straightening the world? Straighten yourself. If each one is good and does good, the world becomes good.

But, Swamiji, on account of that non-violence, India was divided and the two parts are hating each other.

The principle is not at fault; the people had no faith in it. It was just an external decoration. Moreover, geographical nearness has nothing to do with the nearness of the heart. We must be 'dear' to each other, however 'far' we are, geographically. Be near and dear, be far and dear - that is the duty of man. All must be loved and adored as temples, where God is installed.

When will this individualism, Vyaktitwam, disappear, Swamiji?

It will disappear when the *Vyakti* (individual energy), when the bulb knows that it shines through the same current that illumines all the other bulbs, whatever the colour or size.

Why does not Hinduism establish proselytising missions, Swami?

The reason is, Hinduism has no boundaries, or limits. It is only when you have limits that you try to overstep them and try to bring those beyond into the fold. It has no aliens. All are pilgrims trudging along the same road, towards the same shrine - their paces may be different, but their goal is the same.

How can we acquire Ananda (Spiritual Bliss), Swamiji?

Ananda is not something you can acquire or procure from somewhere, outside you, or from someone other than you. It is in you, all the time, it is your genuine nature. You are *Ananda*. That is why I address you as *Anandaswaroopa*. When you experience *Ananda*, it is *Prapta-prapti* (getting the already got), not *aprapta-prapti* (getting the not-got). This gentleman here, with a book, needs, let us say, five shillings urgently; he asks the doctor sitting by his side to lend him the sum. The doctor agrees, but even as he is saying so, he takes the book casually into his hand and turning over the pages, he finds between the leaves a five-shilling note! He gives it back to the owner, saying, "You do not need a loan, now; this is yours; you had it all this while; only, you did not know you had it." This is 'getting-the-already-got'. *Ananda* is got like this. The *Guru* or Spiritual Master or Preceptor reveals to you the treasure of *Ananda*, which you had, but which you had forgotten or neglected or discarded or never knew of.

We are trying our best, Swami, to know the source of Ananda, but this Adhi, Vyadhi, and Upadhi do not end and we have no peace.

Do not put the three things together, for the *Adhi* and the *Vyadhi* affect only the *Upadhi* (Physical body); they cannot affect 'you', who are only residents in the *upadhi*. *Adhi* means 'mental pain' and *Vyadhi* means 'bodily pain'; both affect but the health.

How can your car be 'you'? Meditate on this truth and by practice, make that truth evident in your consciousness at all times. Then, *Adhi* and *Vyadhi* will not affect you. They will pass harmlessly by.

Swamiji, our children ask us about God; they argue that there is no God. They ask us to prove to them the value of religion. What shall we do?

Yes. Children are growing up in an atmosphere of irreverence, competition, and pride. They do not observe their parents praying to God or worshipping Him or adoring Him in gratitude for all the favours received. Show them that religion has made you more peaceful and happy, more courageous and independent, more open-minded and liberal - then, they will themselves realise the value of religion. Children start questioning like this, about the age of 14 or 15, isn't it? What have you done all the 14 or 15 years, to instil faith, humility, reverence, and fear of sin in them? It is in the home through the mother, the father, the elders, that the children learn these lessons. They are to be shaped into perfection, as a sculptor shapes boulders into an inspiring image of a saint or sage or even God. Parents and the teachers in schools have to shoulder this responsibility.

But, Swamiji, teachers are paid such low salaries!

That is no reason why they should shirk their responsibility; once they have agreed to serve as teachers, they should not play false to the trust imposed upon them and accepted by them. That will be treason to the children. They should not do something, which they teach their pupils not to do. The parents must strengthen and supplement the teachings, which the schools impart, by their behaviour and conversation at home. There must be co-ordinated endeavour by parents, teachers, and leaders of society to imbue the children with ideals of love and service.

Swamiji, we have now got in You the supreme Doctor. Give us all some medicine to cure our ills.

How can a doctor give one medicine for all? Each one has to be diagnosed separately and given the medicine he needs. Is it not? Four patients may complain of stomach-ache, but the ache may be caused by indigestion or gastric trouble or local injury or appendicitis. I shall meet you individually and give you the medicine and advice you need.

4.

The I Of All I's

(Speech at Public Meeting in Kampala - 7-7-1968)

Love God; that love alone gives access to the source of love. Through love, one can merge in the ocean of love, which is God. Love cures all pettiness, all hate, all grief. Love loosens bonds and saves man from the cycle of birth and death. Love establishes contact with all living beings, a contact of heart with heart. Seen through the eye of love, all beings are filled with divinity and the whole world is one vast kith and kin.

Man is born in society, he is bred in society, he is influenced by society and he in turn, influences society. The interaction is consistent and strong. No man can lead an independent life; his life is bound by the standards, modes, and behaviour patterns of the society into which he is born. The *deha* and the *desha* are inextricably bound together; the body is one encasement, the country is another for the spirit of man. Individual effort is often a failure, but united effort wins success. A single blade of grass is a weak, contemptible thing; but twist a number of them together, it forms a rope, strong enough to bind a rogue elephant. One man is a weakling; many bound together by love into a strong combination can achieve great things.

Everyone in the world craves for security and peace, joy and happiness. But, each believes these can be won from the nature around him. He considers the external world to be eternal and full of value. But, he goes about the world, like a letter, bearing neither the 'from' address, nor the 'to' address. The letter is sent to the office known as the 'dead letter' office. Man too goes from death to birth and then, on to death, for he knows neither the place from which he came, nor the place to which he is going. He simply wastes his life in eating, drinking, playing, and resting. This human existence, these few years of life on this world as man, endowed with rare qualities of head and heart, has been earned by a series of endeavour-filled lives as members of inferior species; that victory is now reduced to ashes by this sloth and this ignorance.

A merchant was once being ferried across a broad river in floods, by a boatman. While crossing, the merchant accosted the boatman and asked him, "Hello, what o'clock is it now?" The man said he had no watch and he did not know. This drew upon him a big tirade, that he was unfashionable, that he was not flowing with the current of the times, that even persons who did not know how to read a watch must have one round the wrist, and that without such a sign of civilisation on the wrist, life is as bad as a quarter lost. A few minutes later, he asked the boatman, who was slowly paddling along, "Hello, what is the latest news?" When the poor fellow declared that he had no habit of reading newspapers, the merchant condemned him for that also and declared that his life was as bad as half lost. So too, when the boatman accepted that he had no transistor radio with him, to while away his time, the merchant laughed and said that, the boatman had wasted and lost three quarters of his life. Meanwhile, a heavy storm was brewing; the sky darkened all of a sudden and a heavy downpour was expected every moment; the flooded river developed high waves and the boat began to roll ominously. Now, it was the boatman's turn to ask a question, "Do you know how to swim?" The merchant, already deep in fear, replied, "No." "In that case," said the boatman, "your entire life is lost."

Of what avail are other skills, if one does not know how to swim over the waves of joy and grief, of pleasure and pain, and profit and loss? One must know the art of being fully at ease, perfectly calm and unaffected, unruffled, whatever may happen to the body or the senses or the mind, for they are all inert, while the inner 'I' alone is 'Intelligence, conscious of itself.' Learn first the skill of internal peace, the art of being always aware of the *Atma* as the real Reality, and then you can gyrate in the world as much and as safely as you want.

Now, man suffers from one illness and he resorts to remedies that can cure another. Diagnose yourself, discover the root cause, and apply the proper remedy - that is the course for the wise. Sow the seeds of *Prema* or love in the well-prepared soil of the heart; let them grow and yield the blossoms of *sahana*, or fortitude; later, you are assured of the fruit, *Shanti* or Peace. This is the task, this is the duty, this is the vow.

Forms of worship or adoration or address may be different, but all religions strive towards the same goal. Just as the same blood stream circulates in all the limbs of the body, the same divine principle activates the entire universe. Visualise it and love all. This is implied in the statement, fatherhood of God and brotherhood of man. Do not take to the business of living too seriously and forget this truth in the struggle that it involves. Life is a newspaper, which is to be read casually and thrown aside. The very next day, it becomes waste paper. So too, life here is worth only a casual perusal, do not attempt to read it again. One birth is enough to end all births. Fix attention on the individual; differences raise their ugly head. Fix attention on the collective, identity will be evident. If you concentrate on the labels like Hindu, Christian, Muslim, Parsi, Buddhist, then you will develop pride or contempt or appreciation and calumny. But, if you feel the unity of the essence, then it will be all love and co-operation. Do not emphasise distinction and difference; emphasise the unity. Go into the deeper significances, the inner meanings of religious symbols, of rites and rituals. The outer forms are in accordance with the needs of the place, time, and person. Just as among you, who have gathered here, there are some, who relish one type of sweetmeat and others, who relish other types, the different names and forms are to satisfy the tastes of different tongues, but all are sweet, sweetened by the same substance, Sugar-God.

Those, who carp and criticise and ask questions, like, "If there is God, where is He?" "Of what form is He?" etc., have not proceeded beyond the first letters of the alphabet of spiritual inquiry and practice. It is only when the entire alphabet is mastered that words, sentences, and paragraphs and the entire book can be read and understood.

Unless you know the I, how can you know the I of all I's, God, the I that makes every I experience the I-ness? It is the fog of ignorance that hides from your consciousness this I of all I's. It is called *maya*, in Hindu philosophy. In the Hindu scripture, *maya* is designated as danseuse, who by her charms deludes the intellect, a *Nartaki*. So, the best way to overcome the charms and be free from the enchantment, is to immerse yourself in *Kirtan*, glorification of God. That will keep the vision clear of material desire and straight on the sublime and the supreme. This is the *Radha-tatwa*, the principle that was the motive-power of the life of Radha, famous as the nearest of Krishna's devotees. Radha was *dhara* (a continuous stream) of Godward flow; she had no spark of consciousness of anything other than God.

This fundamental ignorance, this basic delusion is like coal, dark, dirty. But, it can be made bright, shining, and useful; it can be so made by keeping it in contact with live cinders and vigorous fanning; then, the black, dirty coal will become resplendent and shining. The contact with cinders is 'the company' that one has to seek and submerge oneself in; the 'fanning' is the disciplinary practices that one has to go through.

You are all caskets of divine love. Spread it, share it with all. And, never allow a single moment to go waste. Express that love in acts of service, words of sympathy, thoughts of compassion. Do not develop undue attachment to the world of to worldly comfort. Just as when you awake, you know that the dream, in which you experienced a chain of events that must have taken place over many years, was but a matter of minutes. When you awake into *Gnyana* or Supreme wisdom, after this 'dream' of 'years of living', you will realise that this is but a quick, transient, tawdry affair. Be always full of joy, so that when death calls, you can quit in the fullness of joy with a smile and not in a whimper. The photographer warns us to be ready and steady before he clicks, but God gives no warning signal before the click of death, so that you can get ready and steady in time. Joy can come only through detachment and devotion to a higher purpose, dedication to a noble endeavour. I bless you that you may so shape your lives and activities that this supreme joy and peace will be ever with you.

5.

The Only Raft

(Speech at a Public Meeting in Kampala, 8-7-1968)

O tongue, who seeks the sweet
Come, let me whisper a secret to thee;
The sweetest taste does spring within
Each sacred Name of God.

Life on Earth is a vast, deep ocean, ever restless with the waves of joy and grief, of loss and gain, and the swirling currents of desire, the whirlpools of passions, and the storms of greed and hate. To cross the ocean, the only raft is a heart filled with the Love of God. Man is born for a higher destiny. He should not fritter his life away in low pursuits and vulgar avocations. His destiny is to know the Truth and live in it, by it, and for it. The Truth alone can make him free, bold, and glad. If he is not prompted by this high purpose, life is a waste, a mere tossing on the waves, for the sea of life is never calm. Man seeks to get contentment and joy, by subjugating nature to his fragile will. But, all his efforts to establish mastery over *Prakriti* or nature, or command it or employ it for personal aggrandizement are bound to fail, are bound to recoil on man, with deadly effect. In India, the story of the Ramayana is widely known. In that story, Ravana coveted Sita, the daughter of the earth, that is to say, nature Herself. He did not have any affection for Rama, the Lord of nature (Sita); he sought to gain nature, instead of the master of nature; the penalty he paid was terrific; he perished amidst the ruins of the vast empire he had laboriously built up, amidst the corpses of the people, who had given him unswerving loyalty. Ravana was a great scholar; he had reached the high pinnacle of asceticism and won many supernatural powers, but since he did not bend before the master of *Prakrithi*, of the universe, of nature, he suffered irreparable damnation.

When his steps are towards God, man has no reason to fear; but, when they are turned away from Him, fear haunts him at every turn. That is the source of the highest joy. People yearn for joy and believe they can derive it through the objective world that can be cognised by the senses. No one knows that nature is the vesture of God; there is nothing real, except He. When the morning sun is above the horizon and you walk away from it, towards the west, your long shadow marches before you. That shadow is *maya*, which deludes and hides the Truth. To disregard and discard *maya*, you have to turn sunwards. Then, the shadow falls behind you. The Sun is described as the source of reason and intelligence. When the Sun climbs higher and higher, the shadow you cast becomes smaller and smaller, until at last, when He is right on top of you, the shadow (*maya*) crouches at your feet, surrendering to you and you can trample on it. So too, when your intellect is clarified, *maya* cannot harm you and cast its evil spell on you.

The *Gayatri* hymn of the Vedas, recited thrice a day by millions, asks for the awakening of the intellect, so that when it brightens, the smog delusion is melted. Then, the waves of decision and indecision that confuse and confound are stilled. This is the process of *Yoga*, or *Chittavritti nirodha*, as defined by the Sage Patanjali, the stoppage of the wanderings of the mind, which is but another name for a bundle of desires. *Bhakti* is also a *Yoga*, a process of mental training, by which the mind is transformed into an instrument of God. *Bhakti* or devotion has assumed the shape of a ritual, like turning the beads of the rosary, sitting a specified number of hours before the image, offering incense, waving lights, bell-ringing, dipping in rivers or climbing hills. These are acts that quieten some urges and no more. *Bhakti* is not some uniform clothing that can be put on and off, as the occasion demands. The constables here, while on duty, wear their uniforms and medals and ribbons while on duty, but when they go home, they take it off and wear other items of dress. Devotion is not a uniform you wear when you come for meetings like this, or go to a temple or house of God or when you are on a pilgrimage, a uniform you discard when you relapse into normalcy.

Today, man dabbles in *Yoga* (devotional practices) in the mornings, revels in *Bhoga* (festivity and luxury, catering to the senses) during the day and tosses about in *roga* (disease) during the night. *Bhakti* is not to be indulged in during certain hours of the day, to be superseded by other more fashionable attractions, when they press upon the attention. It is a continuous elevating bent of mind, a habit of thought, a way of living. It must be loyally adhered to, whatever may happen, dishonour, distress, despair, deprivation.

The devotee is deeply aware of the transitoriness of earthly victories. He sees God everywhere, in all beings. He has unbounded equanimity. He will not slide from Truth, Morality, Equanimity, and Love, whatever the temptation. He knows that the God he adores is the indweller of all, that He answers the prayers of all people in all languages. He has no trace of anger; he is not worried at all. When the teeth bite the tongue, does anyone get angry with the hard, sharp teeth for cutting into the soft tongue? Does anyone break the teeth in vengeance for th wrong? No. Because, the teeth and the tongue are both of the same person. So too, the biter and the bite are both of the same body; they are not two, distinct entities. Feel that oneness and avoid hate.

When attention is focussed on the aspirations that are common to all, the joys and griefs that are shared by all, he becomes kin to everyone. God is on the lookout for this inner vision; He bless those, whose hearts can take in all His children. He does not care for external pomp and show.

A rich merchant was having for his daily worship a golden Ganesh, weighing 20 tolas. He got a mouse of Gold, weighing 20 tolas, as the vehicle for Ganesh and a golden chair weighing 20 tolas, for placing Ganesh on. As days passed, penury overwhelmed him and he had to sell the image, the mouse, and the chair. So, he took them to a goldsmith, who offered to purchase all three at a certain uniform price of so many rupees per tola. The man was shocked that the image of the God and the chair were being evaluated alike. But, the goldsmith was paying for the gold, not for the form which the gold was in. So too, God values the gold in you, not the outer expressions of that gold. He looks for faith and sincerity, virtue and earnestness in *Sadhana*, not outer conformity and correctitude.

Even in this distant Kampala, you might know the Indian 'idli', which is eaten with a dish called '*Sambar*'. *Sambar* is a thickish soup prepared with *dal*, vegetables, tamarind, and salt, with some spices thrown in. Now, you may have the very best *dal*, the very best vegetables, the sourest tamarind fruit, and high class of salt and spices. But, if '*sambar*' is cooked in a copper vessel, untinned, the dish will turn out highly poisonous. Similarly, you may do *japam* for hours, or *bhajan* for days, or asceticism for years, or fasts, vigils, and vows for a lifetime; if the heart is not lined with Love, all the effort will turn into dust.

You must first have a clear understanding of the nature of the goal, its grandeur, its glory. Then, that understanding itself will prompt you. The Universal of which you are a unit, is egoless, pure, true, and everlasting. Contemplate on it and your innate egolessness, truth, purity, and eternality will become manifest. This handkerchief is white; when it is covered with dirt and the whiteness is impaired, the washerman takes it and as we say, "makes it white." But, he does not 'make' it white; whiteness is its innate characteristic. So too, *Sadhana* does not make the *Atma* pure, true, eternal, and egoless. Those are its real characteristics.

You may have accumulated wealth, acquired vast scholarship, and achieved health and strength. But, unless you have a vision of the supreme Godhead and an aspiration to be established in that vision, all this is just lumber. In India, people know the celebrated epic, the Mahabharata, which describes a war between the Kauravas and the Pandavas. The Kauravas had vast, financial, military, and human resources. They approached the Lord, Krishna, and were content to receive from Him a large army and a huge quantity of weapons. The Pandavas, however, sought from Him only His grace and the Lord said He will be on their side, alone and unarmed. The Kauravas were defeated to the uttermost; the Pandavas won an empire and eternal fame. If God is on your side, you have the whole world in your hold. This is the lesson taught in the great Hindu scripture, "Give up all bonds of rights and duty; surrender unreservedly to Me. I shall guard you from sin and liberate you from the cycle of birth and death, into the reality of everlasting joy."

You talk in terms of shillings in Kampala. Well, in India, a rupee is equal to a hundred *paise*. Suppose a man has a hundred rupees all in paise, he will have then a heavy load of 10,000 *paise*; he may not know where he can keep the pile. If he is able to get a hundred-rupee-note in exchange for the pile, he will be happy and free. Each worry is a *paisa*; each anxiety is a *paisa*. Take all the 10,000 of them to God and get from Him the hundred-rupee-note, His grace. Surrender all your joys and sorrows to Him. Of course, even the *paise* have to be genuine coins of the realm. He will reject the counterfeit ones. When you secure His grace in return for the vast quantity of sorrow and grief, you are light and free.

Freedom and light are what man needs most; he needs them more than even breath. This is the reason why he is miserable when bound and in the dark. A fish may be placed in a beautiful bowl of gold, studded with brilliant, precious stones, but it will struggle frantically, to reach its native home, water. Man too yearns frantically to escape from this stone-studded world of sensual attractions to God, who is his home, *Ananda*, which is his element. He seeks it up in the sky, down in the bowels of the earth. But, all the time, it lies in his own heart. He can tap the spring of joy, if he knows how to delve into it, in the silence of deep meditation. His consummation consists in his being crowned as emperor of his inner dominion. That is the triumph, which is his due, the 'Consecration' for which he has come in mortal flesh. Few are aware of this Ascent, which is his prize.

There was an emperor, whose treasury was full, whose army was unbeatable, whose minsters were wise, whose subjects were happy and loyal. He marched against his neighbour and through a trick of fate, was defeated and had to withdraw. While withdrawing, he fell ill; his eminent physicians could not save him. They said, it was a matter of minutes for him to meet his end. So, he called his trusted minister to his bedside and gave him instructions that his body should be conveyed to the cemetery, wound up in white cloth, with the two hands raised aloft and the palms spread open, for all to see. The minister asked him what explanation he was to give the people, who might blame him for treating his body in that absurd manner. The king said, "Tell them that I wanted them to know that their emperor is departing from this world, with empty hands, that all that he earned and amassed, he is leaving behind, that everyone must know the evanescence of worldly wealth, power, and fame." One carries with him into the world beyond only the good that he has done; one is burdened with the consequences of the evil that one has done, even beyond the world. That is all. Even the body so fondly fostered has to be cast into flames or thrown into the grave.

Many believe that *Sadhana* and spiritual discipline are to be taken up only during old age. This is a wrong attitude. Earn the reward that awaits you, while you are strong, healthy, and young. It is never too soon to begin. The first step in *Sadhana* is the control of the tongue. Talk only as much or as little as is essential. Make that talk, as sweet and pleasant as you can. Do not talk ill of others; do not see evil in others. The tongue, the eye, the ear, the hand, and the mind should all be trained to avoid evil. If these are kept clean, the grace of God will descend on the person. He will be happy here and hereafter. God will materialise Himself before him and manifest Himself within him.

Childhood, boyhood, youth, and old age are stages, through which the body passes in its natural course. Each stage is short and transforms itself into the next without notice. Do not believe that youth can be retained indefinitely and develop a fascination for the passions, if aroused. Whenever the flesh urges you to fall into falsehood, stand up bravely; do not yield. Stand firm, against the temptation. Keep good company. When dust seeks the company of air, it rises up to the sky; when it seeks the company of water, it is carried into the deep hollows. When iron keeps company with fire, it becomes bright and pure; when it joins the company of the earth, it rusts and soon becomes dust. When the individual is strong and bold, the family is prosperous; when the villages are happy, the country is secure and strong; when countries are strong and happy, the world is prosperous and full of joy.

There is an intimate relationship between the atmosphere, the clouds that roam through it, the rain that falls from them, the crops that those rains feed, the food that the crops provide, the character that the food induces in the persons consuming it, and the attitude of the nation composed of such persons. Food feeds the head; it should be such that the head is made clear and calm; the head should be used to know God. If you sing aloud the glory of God and fill the atmosphere with divine adoration, the clouds will pour the sanctity through rain on the fields; the crops will take it up and sanctify the food; the food will induce divine urges in man. This is the main message of mine. This is the service that each can do, to himself and others.

Man is divine; he can purify himself into perfect divinity. *Nara* can evolve into *Narayana*; *manava* can rise to the status of *Madhava*; *Jana* can all become *Janardhana*, as the saying goes. The process of *Dhyana* (Meditation) if taken up with enthusiasm and followed through with faith, can confer this transformation. As regards the technique of *Dhyanam*, different teachers and trainers give different forms of advice. But, I shall give you now the most universal and the most effective form. This is the very first step in spiritual discipline. Set aside a few minutes every day, at first, for this, and later, go on extending the time as and when you feel the bliss that you can get. Let it be in the hours before dawn. This is preferable, because the body is refreshed after sleep and the peregrinations of day time have not impinged on you. Have a lamp with an open flame, steady and straight, or a candle before you. Sit in the *padmasana* posture or any other comfortable *Asana*, in front of the candle. Look on the flame, steadily, for sometime and closing your eyes, try to feel the flame inside you, between your eyebrows; let it slide down into the lotus of your heart, imagine that the petals of the lotus open out, one by one, bathing every thought, feeling, and emotion in the light and so removing darkness from them. There is no space for darkness to hide. The light of the flame becomes wider and brighter. Let it pervade your limbs; now, those limbs can never more deal in dark, suspicious, wicked activities; they have become instruments of light and love. Let the light reach up to the tongue; falsehood vanishes from it. Let it rise up to the eyes and ears, and destroy all the dark desires that infest them, leading you into perverse sights and puerile conversation. Let your head be surcharged with light and all wicked thoughts flee therefrom. Imagine that the light is in you, more and more intensely; let it shine all around you and let the light spread from you, in ever widening circles, taking in your loved ones, your kith and kin, your friends and companions - may your enemies and rivals - strangers, all men and women, wherever they are, all living beings, the entire world.

Since the light illumines all the sense, every day, so deeply and so systematically, a time will soon come when you can no more relish dark and evil sights, yearn for dark and sinister tales, crave for low, harmful, deadening, toxic food and drinks, handle dirty, demeaning things, approach places of ill-fame and injury, or frame evil designs against anyone, anytime. Stay on in that thrill, the thrill of witnessing Light everywhere. If you are adoring God in any form now, try to visualise that form in the all-pervasive light. For, light is God; God is light. In this *Ashanti* (confounding world), you must seek our *Prashanti* (the higher tranquillity); in that *Prashanti*, you must experience the *Prakanti*, the supreme light; that supreme light is *Jyoti*, is sublimated into *Paramjyoti*, the all-embracing Immanent Splendour; in that *Paramjyoti*, the aspirant finally cognises the Universal Eternal Absolute, the *Paramatma*. When light meets light, it is all light. When the individual meets the universal, all is universal. I and I are called We. We and He are only We. There are no two; there is only One, appearing as many.

Do not misuse life in idle, meaningless pursuits. Practise this 'meditation' as I have advised, regularly, every day. At other times, repeat the name of God (any name, fragrant with any of His many majesties), always taking care to be conscious of His might, mercy, and munificence.

I want that you, in Kampala, should gather in groups for *bhajan* and adore God and sing His glory. It is not enough, if you assemble, on those rare occasions, when some *mahatma* or saint or sage comes to town. Whether someone visits or not, you must do this duty to yourself. Meet once a week or oftener, engage yourselves in *bhajan* for some while, read some spiritual book that will inspire you to greater aspirations, meditate for sometime, and depart, refreshed and strengthened. Feed the little lamp of yours with the oil of enthusiasm lent by others. Let the *jyoti* of your heart merge in the universal *jyoti*. You can also, wherever possible, move along the streets, singing in chorus, the Name of God, the Glory of God, in any Form, in all Forms. This is called *Nagara-sankeertan* in India; it awakens in all the consciousness that all are living in the shadow of God. It is done before dawn and so, the day starts for all, who participate and all, who hear, with the paean of praise for the Giver of Gifts.

Embodiments of Love! Cultivate the quality of love, pure, unsullied by selfish desire; share that love with all, people of all colours and creeds and nationalities. The same, intense craving for God that you are now having is expressed in another language, in another style, in another creed. Sharing heightens *Ananda*; holding back produces grief.

Stagnant water is rendered foul; flowing waters are pure and clear. Love is *Ananda*; Love is power; Love is light; Love is God.

I shall come to you again, next year, and stay longer. I shall be happy, if each one of you becomes by then a lamp of love, shedding virtue and purity all around you.

6.

Serve Thy Self

(Talk with delegates from Kampala, Jinja, Nairobi, Mbale, Eldoret, Nakuru, etc., 9-7-1968)

You must have rules and regulations and constitutions; but, they must help you do things in a smoother way; they should not hinder, or throw hurdles. They are like the bunds that keep the stream flowing straight towards the sea. If you have strong faith in the value of the task you are engaged in and if you are sincere in the service that you do, then the rules are not so important. Remember that the service of others is a duty you owe to yourself, for you really need the joy that the service gives. That joy is something beyond words.

What you call 'service' to others is fundamentally 'service' to your own self. You serve yourselves best, when you serve others best. When you relieve the distress of others, you are winning relief from your own distress.

A cow was once caught in a deep morass and she was struggling desperately to extricate herself. The slush was mercilessly dragging her into its depths. The ragamuffins of the village were enjoying the mortal struggle, which they witnessed gleefully, cheering the helpless animal when it floundered deeper and deeper. Just then, a monk, who was passing along that road, saw the plight of the poor cow; he jumped into the bog, without a second thought; he dived into the mire and rose with the cow upon his hefty shoulders. He carried her safe out of the morass and placed her on her legs, on dry land. Then, he quietly resumed his journey.

The village lads jeered at him, for he had spoiled their fun. They asked him why he had risked his life so stupidly; they spoke cynically of his great act of 'service'. The monk replied, "I did not help the cow; I only helped myself. I felt the terribly agony of the cow in my own heart. I had to seek relief. I could not but jump in and save her. I am now happy. My pain has gone."

When you find that others are suffering or in pain, you should feel the pain and the suffering as your own and you should remove it, by serving them. Cultivate that sympathy; that is the highest *Sadhana*. The Vedas declare, "*Na karmana, na prajaya, dhanena, tyagenaike amritatwam anasuh,*" "Immortality can be won and experienced neither through the performance of rites, nor through progeny, nor by the accumulation of wealth; it can be won only by renunciation." Give up - give up your comforts, your time, your skills, in order to help others. That is the way to gain immortality.

Man is bound by one of three ropes or *gunas* (peculiar natures). The *Tamasic* chain of dull deleterious desires, which lead him to sloth, sensualism, and sin (this can be called an iron chain), the *Rajasic* chain of ambition and acquisitiveness, of competition, and pride (this can be called the copper chain), and the *Satwic* chain of humility and simplicity, which make him good and virtuous (this too is a chain, albeit a golden chain). All three bind man; man has to become pure, with no characteristics in his make-up. The word *guna* means a rope and it does bind. This is its justification. You cannot complain against it for that. To escape from these chains that bind him, man has to adopt one of the two stratagems; (I) He can immerse himself in the feeling, *Dasoham*, I am the servant, and reduce his size, steadily, until the chain falls off and he escapes. This is the path of the *Bhakta*, the *Dasa*, the servant, of laying the 'I' at the Feet of the Almighty, of unreserved surrender, of Prahlada, who had no will or thought of his own. Or, (II) he can expand himself with the feeling, *Shivoham*, I am Shiva, I am divine, I am the eternal, the Absolute; he becomes so vast, so pervasive, so grand that no chain can contain him; it snaps and he is free.

Imagine God as resident in the top floor of a high mansion. The stairs, by which alone you can reach Him, are guarded by a fierce dog - *maya*. *Maya* is the monster of ignorance, which deludes you into the belief that the transitory is eternal and that the eternal is non-existent. The dog will not harm you, if the Master comes down in response to your prayers and takes you up along with Him. This is what the *Bhakta* does. He pleads, he prays, he yearns and God comes down for his sake and showers grace on him. The *Bhakta* is like the kitten, which mews piteously, sitting in one place; the cat hurries towards it and lifts it gently with its teeth, and removes it to a place of safety. This is the reason why *Bhakti* is often referred to as the kitten-way to God. Another method of reaching the master in the mansion is to become an exact prototype of the master, so that the dog believes you to be the Master Himself. Know the master; you become the master. *Brahmavid Brahmaiva bhavati*: He, who knows *Brahman*, becomes *Brahmam*. The *Gnyani*, who knows that he is the eternal absolute, becomes the Absolute. *Maya* dare not delude him anymore. This is a hard path, where the pilgrim has to trudge alone. He is like the young monkey, which holds fast the mother, while she leaps from branch to branch. There is no room here for the grace of the mother. This is therefore referred to as the 'baby-monkey-way'.

Detachment is the very first step, whether it is *Bhakti* or *Gnyana*. Man saves himself by his own resolute efforts; other can only point the way. Harischandra, the Emperor, who in his determination to stick to truth, lost his empire, his freedom, and his family, had at last to serve as a watchman in a crematorium. When he found corpses being burnt all around him, he realised that the self alone is the friend of the self, the self alone is the foe. Parents, husband, wife, kith, and kin, children are all temporary, transient supporters or dependents. Your only friend is yourself; all others have some motive or other in befriending you.

A young man was going daily to a preceptor, who lived on the outskirts of the town. He received from him lessons on spiritual regeneration. He returned at nightfall to his own home. One evening, however, the master required him to stay on, but the youth protested that his absence at home, even for a single night would plunge his parents and wife in unconsolable grief. The guru told him that a person loves another for his own sake, that no person loves another more than he loves his own self. But, the young man was not convinced; he said, his parents and his wife were overwhelmingly attached to him and that they would not survive, if anything happened to him. The guru said, "We shall find that out." He asked him to swallow a pill that he gave him, as soon as he reached home; he said, the pill would make him fall as if dead, though he could hear and understand all that happened around him.

When he took the pill as directed and slithered on the floor, the parents screamed in agony. The wife lamented loudly. The neighbours came in large numbers, but who could allay their anguish? Suddenly, the Preceptor appeared on the scene and learning the reason for the commotion, he said that the young man could be saved by a simple remedy. He asked for a glass of water; he walked three times round the prostrate body with the glass in his hand and declared, "Now, whoever wants to save this young man can do so; drink this glass of water, then, the person, who drinks it, will die and the young man will come back to life!" He asked the mother to drink it, but she said she had other children to look after, a daughter whose marriage had to be fixed, another who was enciente and so, she retreated from the place into a distant corner. The father too had his excuses; the wife was the only child of her parents and she did not propose to cause them grief. No one of them was ready to sacrifice their lives to save the son. They confabulated together for sometime and came forward with a suggestion, "Revered guru. We shall build a magnificent tomb for you and conduct worship thereon, in memory of your great act of sacrifice. Please drink the water and bring our son back to life!" The son then rose and since he knew that what the guru said was true, he left hearth and home and became a recluse, under the preceptor.

You must also develop the feeling of non-attachment. Be attached to the work, but not to the fruit. Leave it to the grace of God. He prompted the work, He made it possible. Let Him accept the fruit thereof. These poles carrying street lamps - they illumine themselves and illumine the streets also. So too, if you live a life of love and truth, you will be lit and you will shed light around you, to all who come near you.

Get together like-minded people and arrange for *bhajan* sessions, at least once a week; arrange also, readings from religious scriptures or discourses on spiritual subjects, at least once a month. Fill your time with good works, good thoughts, and good reading. Form the nucleus of 'good company' in your town or village and keep it well-knit and steady.

At Dharmakshetra in Bombay, the International Centre of Sathya Sai Organisations is established and you can keep in touch with it, for advice and guidance. Here, in East Africa, it is now proposed to have one Sathya Sai Seva Samiti, at Kampala, Uganda, charged with the duty of guiding and advising all organisations here, for Kenya. Tanzania and Uganda, there will be separate organisations with Vice-Chairmen and Secretaries, functioning from Nairobi, Dar-es-Salaam, and Kampala. They will train volunteers and *bhajan* leaders, promote *Nagarsankeertans*, and sponsor various service activities, like medical and legal relief among the Africans and Indians, as far as their human resources permit. They must also celebrate the festivals and holy days of all religions, with equal fervour; any crop that feeds man needs care and attention. So too, any faith that elevates man must be adored.

7.

Science Of Surrender

(Discourse at the gathering of Sadhakas and spiritual aspirants, Kampala, 9-7-1968)

Swamiji, it is said that the darshan of Mahatmas rids one of the evil effects of past Karma; is that true?

When the consequences of *Karma* are wiped off, evil effects as well as good effects will disappear; the fire of *Gnyana* will not distinguish the good from the bad; both are to be transcended; both are binding and transitory. And, by *darshan* is meant adoration, obedience, acceptance; it is to be followed by *pariprashna* and seva: inquiry and service. Why, one can get rid of the effects of past *Karma*, if *Karma* or Action is done with no sense of 'I' or 'mine'. Once a man beat off a cow that strayed into his well-tended garden and ate off a few plants; the blows were so severe that the cow died and when people charged him with the crime, he said, "I did not kill it; it is God's will that it should die, as a consequence of the blow. How could I help it?" The next day, God Himself entered the garden as a visitor and asked him, "This looks lovely; who planted these and tended them so lovingly?" The man came forward and said, "I planted them; I watered them; I tended; I fostered," I, I, I. When it is something praiseworthy, 'I' did it; when it is something blameworthy, God did it! You must be consistent; say I for both or God for both.

Can we modify the effects of Karma?

You can, by using your intelligence. *Karma* or acts of past births are accumulated and heaped as a big burden called *Sanchita*; out of this accumulation, a portion is taken for consumption at a time, this is called *prarabdha* (that, which is being spent out). With a little intelligence, you can consume it in a manner that conduces to your welfare and promotes your progress. You may have to cook and consume a certain quantity of rice; nothing prevents you from making tasty dishes out of it and guarding your health in the process.

Can anyone escape Karma?

No; breathing itself is an action. God Himself assumes *Karma*, though He is sovereign over all. And, why should you escape it? Doing work in a dedicatory spirit gives such joy and contentment, that once you start that type of *Karma*, you will never like to give it up. Have the attitude that you are but an instrument in His hands, behaving as He declares, as He wills. Then, you have escaped *Karma*, for you are not the doer. It is He, who does all the acts. This is the 'surrender' that the Gita teaches.

What are we to surrender, Swamiji?

Surrender the 'I'. The cobra is dreadful, because it has two poisonous fangs. Man too has two poisonous fangs: 'I' and 'Mine' - *Aham-kara* and *Mamakara*. Pluck the fangs out and you can handle the cobra as you like, go about as a snake-charmer, and earn a livelihood thereby. So too, when 'I' and 'MINE' are removed, man is no longer harmful to himself and others. Vivekananda said that he did not want to become sugar (merge in *Brahmam*); he desired to be the ant that consumes the sugar (the *Gnyani*, who revels in the inexpressible sweetness of *Brahma*-consciousness). The Gita speaks of *Mokshasanyasa*, the renunciation of even the desire, Liberation. Be born, do good, be good, serve God, and godmen. That is a commendable desire. Use the talents you are endowed with: intelligence, discriminating faculty, moral sense, a warning conscience, ability to stand apart as a witness with no attachment.

Shiva is described as having ash smeared all over His Body; You are said to be an Avatar of Shiva; how is it that You do not wear it, but only give it to all?

You do not know the meaning of the word *vibhuti* that is used to describe the ash that Shiva is supposed to have on His Body. You take the meaning that suits you. *vibhuti* means glory, splendour, magnificence, superhuman faculties. Shiva is enveloped in that *vibhuti* - that is what the Vedas say; not that He has ash smeared all over Him! And, when I give *vibhuti* or Ash, it is a reminder of the ultimate, the final and unchangeable thing, into which everything reduces itself. All things become ash and ash becomes nothing else. Produced by *vibhuti*, it is also useful to convey a lesson.

Swamiji, you have announced Yourself as the Avatar of the Sai Baba of Shirdi; how can we get fixed in that faith?

You have not known that Baba; nor do you know this Baba. How then can you argue on this point? Leave it to those, who are competent. Be satisfied with the chance you have secured; make the best of the chance, while you may. As a matter of actual fact, all are incarnations of God. Every *manava* is destined to become *Madhava*; every man will one day become God, just as every river becomes the ocean, when it flows into it.

Is it true that we have had many births previous to this?

Of course, it is true. The Sage Markanda once asked Narada, "I have been practising austerities, since sixty years, but I could not win the boon of God-realisation. That boy, Dhruva, a mere six year old child, spent just five months in austerity and God appeared before him and granted his desires. This is very unjust." But, Narada replied, "A slab of stone breaks into two, when a child gives a hammer stroke. The same slab did not break for twenty hammerstrokes from a hefty hand, administered just previous to the twenty-first. Why? The slab broke as a result of the cumulative effect of all blows, twenty then and one now. So too, Dhruva had years of austerity then, in previous births, and just five months of it in this birth." But, you may ask, "If we had lives previous to this, why do we not remember the events?" Do you remember the events of this life, at least? All the events? Krishna asked Arjuna, "Ten years ago, on the Full Moon Day of the month *Magha*, where exactly where you?" Arjuna could not recall the place. For, it had no significance for him. He could, however, recall the date when he married the sister of Krishna, for that was a happy event he would not forget. There are no significant events in the past life and so, you do not remember any. But, God is concerned with all; so, He remembers all.

Can the study of the Shastras help?

They can, to some extent. They are like signposts. They indicate the direction and perhaps, the distance to be covered. But, they cannot give you an idea of the ups and downs, which you will have to encounter when you go along. Only actual journey will reveal them to you. Engage yourselves in *Karma* in a dedicatory spirit, then you realise that He is omnipotent and omnipresent and the spirit of adoption and surrender becomes well established in you. At last, you will realise that you and He and all else are but One. Thus, *Karma* leads to *Bhakti* and *Bhakti* to *Gnyana*. A cow is tied by a rope to a post; it can graze all round the post, within the radius of the length of rope. When it has grazed that area, the master will untie it and take her to another post or he might lengthen the rope, so that she can graze over a further area. But, first, the allotted area must be grazed, otherwise, there can be no gift of grace.

What happens after death to the individual, Swamiji?

The final thought of the individual decides what form the *Jivi* assumes, when it is born again. Just as the fragrance of a garden of lilies is carried by the breeze, the atmosphere of *gunas* or tendencies and characteristics, which predominates in this life is carried forward into the next. Birth in the next form has to take place very soon, but the interval may be more or less. When you switch on the lights, light comes immediately; when you switch on the fan, it takes time for the fan to whirl fast enough to cool the air. If it is a stove, it takes longer still for the stove to be ready for cooking. Of course, there are many, who are not born again since they merge in the ocean of grace.

But, population does not decrease!

That is because animals and other beings earn the human birth and come in for the great chance.

Perhaps, that is the reason why men are behaving like animals!

Why should you argue that animals, beasts, and birds are bad? Do not talk in an irresponsible manner. Each animal is treading its *dharma*; it does not overstep, or undermine. They have greater co-operation and mutual love than even men. Each has to be judged from the point of view of the equipment and the opportunity. Man can live better, if only he learns from animals. He is degrading himself even lower. When the Lord incarnates, He has as one of His tasks, *"paritranaya sadhoonam,"* the protection of *sadhus*, of beings with quiet innocent natures. Among animals, there are countless sadhus, remember.

Which is the best time of the day for meditation, Swami?

The best time is from 4:30 a.m. or 5 a.m. You are refreshed by sleep; all will be quiet around you. There will be no tension in the body and the mind. Or, you can select 7 p.m. Your day's work will then be over; you will not have a heavy stomach, for you have not had your dinner. If the day's work is not exhaustive, or if it is of a more or less routine nature, you can start meditation about 7 p.m.

Can a person having high blood pressure take up meditation?

Oh, yes. He can. In fact, meditation will cure him; it is soothing and calming. One must continue *Dhyana* or meditation, until one realises that all is suffused with divinity. In the beginning, during meditation, a person might naturally experience some visions and sounds, which spur him on to greater intensity. Later, they become not so prominent and so, enthusiasm should not be allowed to flag. But, why this insistence on a definite time? Wherever you are, wherever you get the chance, you can recite the name of God. When you walk to office and walk back again, have the name on the tongue and the glory in the mind.

How then are we to use the rosary, Swami?

No rosary is needed. Counting the number of times you utter the name may be a source of encouragement, in the beginning; but, after a time, it is unnecessary; it is a needless distraction; it may even cause pride or dejection.

8.

Sharing Of Love

(Address to Volunteers at Kampala, 10-7-1968)

During the last ten days, you have all worked untiringly, in order to provide facilities for thousands of people in this city, to have *darshan* and to attend the meetings and functions. You had no experience of serving as 'volunteers' in such mass gatherings or attending to such huge streams of visitors, but yet, you have done well; this is due to your devotion and enthusiasm, your faith and mutual respect.

Time is the prime basis of existence; from birth to death, you deal with time. You deal in time, use time, misuse time, gain through time, the timeless entity. To win timelessness, in the short time that you have, the grace of God, who is above time, is essential. Birth is a chance to escape further birth; death must be made the final merging. Life is but another name for the effort to know the Truth. And this 'volunteership' is only a means to that end. Why, whatever work is undertaken, with no eye on the benefit therefrom, with intense, selfless love, is a means to attain the Truth. For, service of others removes the attachment to the ego; it also confers joy, joy of a highly satisfying nature.

Hanuman is a good example of the true 'volunteer', the person dedicated to the highest form of service. He had tremendous physical strength, strength to carry mountains on his palm. He had the precious treasure of wisdom, virtue, and grace to an unsurpassed degree. But yet, he was the supreme servant of God. He leaped across the sea and stood defiantly before the throne of Ravana, the mighty ruler of the demons. When he was asked to say who he was, he did not relate his superhuman achievements or his own, personal prowess, but introduced himself as "the servant of Rama!" When Rama asked him once, what he wanted from Him, though he could have got all the things that men covet, he asked only this, "Give me the chance to serve You without intermission."

Krishna too set a great example of service, though He is the *Avatar* of the Lord, the Lord Himself. He is the master of the worlds, the architect, the guide, the guardian. He agreed to act as a common charioteer to Arjuna, He washed the horses, He dressed their wounds. He fed them and harnessed them. All this is to set an example to man, who is ruining himself by developing a swelled head, full of his own importance.

You have now had this exhilarating experience of service. Retain this training and this joy. Develop this and utilise this skill to serve others, not only when big gatherings take place, but even on ordinary days, in out of the way places wherever you are, whatever the chance. Bear with disappointment, slander, criticism, calumny, troubles, worries, whatever people allot to you in their ignorance or envy. Have fortitude and equanimity. Some people may argue with you and challenge you, in rough language, but put up with such; the world is composed of all types of men. Be calm; speak soft and sweet towards them; that will soften their wrath and quieten their tempers.

You must have understood that 'renouncing' your comfort for the sake of another gives great joy. *Tyaga* or renunciation is the path of fulfilment; give up and it will be added unto you. Accumulate and it will be taken away. That is the law of the spirit. Give up and offer what is given up at the lotus feet of God. When you see an old, sick person standing in the sun, when you give your seat to him and yourself stand in his place, you feel as cool as in the shade.

Many of you are in the stage of youth and so, I must warn you against certain pitfalls that youth is liable to. Youth is the time, when it is urgent to regulate, control, and conserve. It is the stage, when temptations are easily victorious; when sensual pleasure casts its net wide; when the eye, the ear, and the tongue drag the mind into ruin. We have men volunteers and lady volunteers and so, when they work at the same place and their work complements each other, it is natural that evil thoughts arise in the ill-disciplined minds. You must discard such thoughts. All are sisters and brothers and so, any evil thought is a sacrilege again at the God, who dwells in all. Fix the mind on God and it will not wander into the woods of sensual pleasures. Sita was in the *Ashokavanam* at Lanka, a lovely garden, full of heavenly blossoms and bowers. But, her mind was afflicted by the agony of separation from Rama, her Lord, and she found no joy in the external charm of that garden. On the other hand, the name Rama that was sung by a monkey (Hanuman) sitting on the tree, an ugly animal strange in that island, that sound gave her the supermost joy. Pleasure and joy reside in the heart, not in the outer charm or beauty or comfort. The mind makes heaven and hell. External charm is a snare, a bubble, a nine days wonder that entices and entraps.

There was a Prince, once, who did not approve as his bride any of the numerous princesses that the King proposed for him. One day, while going on horseback, along the raised bank of a river, his eye fell on a charming maiden, who was proceeding riverwards avoiding the sight of men, for she was a determined recluse desirous of living a retired, ascetic life of spiritual discipline. The Prince fell in love with her and communicated his eagerness to marry her to his father; the king sent for the father of the maiden. He was not in favour of the alliance with the ruler of the kingdom; nor was his daughter amenable to the dictates of any one, however powerful or affectionate, so far as wedlock is concerned. At last, through God's grace, her prayers were answered and she told her father that he could inform the Prince that she was willing to marry him on one condition. He must wait for a week and on the seventh day, he must have a private audience with her. The prince was overjoyed and he could scarce contain himself for the finale of that fateful week.

Meanwhile, (the truth must be told), she consulted a doctor and took daily, for seven days, strong purgative drugs, which exhausted her and reduced her to a skeleton, gaunt and frightening to behold. She collected the excreta in separate vessels, one for each day and transported them, too, cleverly into the hall, where the audience with the Prince was to take place on the seventh day. When the bride was announced, the Prince rushed in to receive the shock of his life. "On account of the excretion of this quantity of foul stuff, I have lost all the charm, which tempted you. Beauty is but a temporary charm, acquired by retaining the things that have thus been removed." When the bride said this, the Prince, too, had his eyes opened. He determined that he will no longer yield to physical attraction or sensual attachments; he renounced earthly things and sought spiritual progress.

Use the body as an instrument; give it only that much of importance. Keep it in good trim. But, do not forget the purpose, the goal, the endeavour. When the higher purpose calls, be prepared to give heart and soul to that. The Gopis of Brindavan were like that. They talked of Krishna, they listened only to talk of Krishna; they thought of Him, dreamt of Him. When they heard the melody of His flute, they fled towards It, whatever the obstacle, whoever came in the way, father, mother, husband, child. Why, even the cows eating grass stood still, entranced by the music of the flute, having the grass in the mouth. 'Calves' drinking milk from the 'udders' stood still, as if they were painting on canvas. That is the depth of concentration, which the Flute induced in them. It is called *Ekagrata* - single-pointedness. The point to which the eye leads is the 'target'; the point to which the ear leads is the 'message'; the point to which the mind leads is 'relish'; the point to which the mind leads is 'God'. It is only diseased eyes that will reach out for other things. It is only the defective ear or the dilapidated tongue that will seek other 'points'. So too, when the mind seeks something other than God, you can be sure it is diseased, defective. When the mind is set on God, it is perfectly healthy. When it is set on the objective world, it is suffering from some kind of phobia or other, some mania, like megalomania. If you do not derive joy from serving your parents or the elders and teachers, then too, you can be sure you are ill in mind. For, such service brings great reward, the reward of the grace of God. Be grateful to those, who gave you this wonderful instrument. Be grateful to those, who brightened the lamp of knowledge in you. Pundarika, a great devotee of Panduranga, was one day massaging the feet of his mother. Then, his Panduranga, the form of God he had installed in his shrine and heart, came in all His splendour and stood before him! What a temptation to give up the service of the mother and rush towards the Feet of His God! But, Pundarika said, "Please wait a few moments. I shall finish this service and then, offer homage to you." He threw a brick for Panduranga to stand upon, for it is the first step in hospitality to offer a seat for the guest!

Pundarika's *guru*, Kabir, told him that one does service to the mother, so that the grace of God can be won, but even then, he did not give up the service in the middle. Such was his steadfastness and his faith.

You must have love for yourself. Of course, there is no one, who is devoid of this; but, they do not know how to express that love. Love must be transmuted into beneficial endeavour, effort to realise the Truth. God is the ocean of love and so, even if our love towards Him is tainted, it does not matter; pour it into the ocean. It will merge in that vast, deep ocean and become divine. Do not wait, until your love is absolutely unselfish and pure. Start offering all the attachment and affection that you have towards objects to the Lotus Feet; He will purify it, He can cleanse it. The very attitude will make them pure. Through *Sadhana*, like *Japam*, *Dhyanam*, and *Namasmarana*, Love is purified as in a filter. The dregs will stay behind; the clean thoughts alone will reach Him.

You have known by experience that a work is better done by co-operation and mutual trust. The eye sees a fruit on a tree, the mind craves for it, the feet walk towards the tree, the back bends, the shoulder swing, the fingers pick up a stone and throw it with good aim at the twig that carries the fruit, the fruit falls to the ground, it is picked up by the fingers and put into the mouth, it is rolled on the tongue, bitten by the teeth, swallowed by the gullet, and digested by the stomach. Now, the stomach in turn, strengthens with the essence of the fruit the gullet, the teeth, the tongue, the fingers, the shoulders, the back, the eye, and the mind. It is all a chain of love and co-operation. Be like this well-connected, well-oriented group.

Love, Peace, and Truth are the very nature of God. Express your divinity through these. That is why I am emphasising *Sathya*, *Dharma*, *Shanti*, and *Prema* as the four pillars of the beautiful mansion of life.

Know that there are springs of Truth, Righteousness, Peace, and Love in all hearts, however mean, or low, or hateful they may appear to you in your dark ignorance. Honour every human being. Sympathise with anyone, who suffers; rejoice with any one, who rejoices. Even after I leave Africa, physically, (I am always here and everywhere), you must carry on the service you did so long. Seek out chances to be serviceable. Also, train yourselves to do service, better and in more fields. I am entrusting you to the Sathya Sai Seva Samitis of Kampala, in Uganda, Nairobi, in Kenya, and Dar-es-Salaam in Tanzania. Under their auspices, very soon, centres of service and training will arise; take those opportunities and prepare for the great task of realising the God within you, through serving the God, the same God, who is in all others, whatever their colour, creed, or country.

Made in the USA
Monee, IL
13 December 2024

73566913R10066